SPLIT SURVIVAL KIT

Discarded

To Megan – for general awesomeness! – R.F.

For all the children and families I've had the pleasure of working with – A.R.

First published in Great Britain in 2022 by Wren & Rook
Text © Ruth Fitzgerald and Angharad Rudkin 2022

The right of Ruth Fitzgerald and Angharad Rudkin to be identified as the authors of this Work has been asserted by them in accordance with the Copyright, Designs & Patents Act 1988.

ISBN: 978 1 5263 6402 9
E-book ISBN: 978 1 5263 6403 6
1 3 5 7 9 10 8 6 4 2

MIX
Paper from responsible sources
FSC® C104740

Wren & Rook
An imprint of
Hachette Children's Group
Part of Hodder & Stoughton
Carmelite House
50 Victoria Embankment
London EC4Y 0DZ

An Hachette UK Company

www.hachette.co.uk
www.hachettechildrens.co.uk

Printed in the United Kingdom

The website addresses (URLs) included in this book were valid at the time of going to press. However, contents or addresses may have changed since the publication of this book. No responsibility for any such changes can be accepted by either the author or the publisher.

Dr Angharad Rudkin
Ruth Fitzgerald

SPLIT
SURVIVAL
KIT

Illustrated by
Stef Murphy

10 STEPS
For coping with
your parents'
separation

wren
&rook

CONTENTS

INTRODUCTION

'As soon as he saw the BIG Boots, Pooh knew that an ADVENTURE was going to happen.'

Narrator, *Winnie the Pooh*

This is an unusual book.

It's not an adventure story, or an exciting mystery, or a book which tells you interesting facts about the lifespan of the leatherback turtle. In fact, most people reading this book probably wish they didn't have to. After all, let's face it, reading about your parents splitting up is never going to be a bundle of laughs. But it's still an important book. Because, although parental separation is really very common, and happens in the families of around a quarter of all children in the UK, for some reason no one ever seems to want to talk about it. There are loads of books about fairies and wizards and football legends, but not many that tell us what to do when our parents won't speak to each other.

Perhaps that's because when people separate or get divorced it usually makes us feel sad, and we think that talking or reading about sad things will make us feel even worse. Best to shove it all under a rock and carry on as if everything is just fine and normal:

'Move along, please. Nothing to see here!'

But if your parents are separating, you'll know it can feel as if you're setting out on a journey you never wanted to make. One day you're cruising along on a calm sea and the next you're hit by a huge wave. Your whole world is being turned upside down and you're out of your depth! You need something solid to hang on to and some help to reach a safe and happy place again.

So, this book aims to do just that. Like a guide for your journey, we're going to help you navigate the rocky waters and the rough terrain to come. We are going to roll back the rock and look at all the messy stuff that's been shoved under there, and then we're going to deal with it. We are going to face up to all the horrible, shouty, door-slamming arguments and the sad, snotty crying. Yes, it happens. We know. We're going to bring it out into the open and talk about how to manage these feelings in ourselves and others. We are also going to look at how to manage all the awkward practical arrangements about schools, houses, holidays and birthdays – the stuff that makes everyone argue and stress. We'll discuss parents, siblings, friends, teachers and step-families, but most of all we'll talk about you. About how you feel, what you're anxious about and what might make you feel better.

Along the way, we'll explain some of the things that go on inside our heads, and show that understanding how our brains work can really help us to figure out why we, or other people, might be thinking or acting in a particular way. We'll give you ideas to help you feel more in control, strategies to help you feel more positive and tactics for getting your voice heard when it seems like no one is listening. We'll also hear about some other young people who've been on the same journey and find out what worked for them. By the end of it we hope the very usable ideas in this book can really help you get through the tough times and step into the future with more strength and confidence.

Getting through a family split is like going on a difficult voyage. No one is going to pretend the way ahead will be easy – it will be hard and there will be bumps and setbacks and obstacles to overcome. If you were an adventurer setting out on a real journey, you'd take a survival kit with items

like a map, a torch and a compass, to help you find your way. For the journey you're on, this book will be like a survival kit – a set of tools to pull out and use when you hit a tough patch. You might want to assemble a few things of your own to help you as we go – like a pen and a
notebook or journal, a chocolate bar (important for extra energy) and, if you can find one, a quiet place to sit, think and read.

What's in this book?

Every chapter in *Split Survival Kit* has lots of different ideas and sections:

※ **Grab a Pen!** For these sections you'll need to write or draw in your journal.

※ **Thinking Differently.** Ways of thinking about a situation that might give you a different way of seeing it.

※ **It Happened to Me.** Real-life stories of young people who've been through parental separations.

※ **Try This.** Activities and ideas.

※ **Dealing With the Feeling.** Exercises to help manage strong emotions.

Although the strategies in the book will help you, there will still be times when you feel very sad, angry or confused, but if you keep moving forward, the difficult times will get fewer and you will navigate the journey and come through stronger and wiser than before.

So perhaps this book is a kind of adventure story after all, except the hero of this book **is you**.

Let's set off ...

The real-life stories included in this book are based on the genuine experiences of real people, but names and details have been changed to protect their privacy.

CHAPTER ONE

HELP! I WANT TO TURN BACK
HOW TO COME TO TERMS WITH WHAT'S HAPPENING

'No matter how **TALL** the mountain is, it cannot block the sun.'

Chinese Proverb

All day long your brain sits in your head doing what it likes to do. Looking after you. Moment by moment it scans the environment for anything that might upset you, injure you or even just cause you to feel slightly uncomfortable. As soon as it detects a possible problem it jumps to attention and pings up a helpful thought into your conscious mind:

You know the sort of thing.

Of course, we don't really notice our brain doing all this stuff – mostly it just gets on with things quietly in the background. Like a ship depends on a captain, to navigate the vessel safely through calm water, choppy waves and even the occasional storm, we depend on our brain to help us cope with the

ups and downs of life without too much of a problem. Which it nearly always does; that is, until something major happens. Like when parents tell you they have decided to separate.

Wham! Life just hit you with a huge wave. Deal with that, Captain Brain!

Whether you had no idea your parents were thinking of parting and you thought everything at home was fine, or whether you've realised it was likely for quite some time, once your parents confirm they are splitting up, it's likely to be a big shock.

Faced with any sort of unknown situation, it's very common for our brain to go into a bit of a panic. After the initial shock, it just wants to protect us from the bad news, so one of the first ideas it pings up is that maybe we can stop the changes happening.

You might find you have some thoughts like this:

 Perhaps there's some way of getting them to fall back in love.

 If me and my sister show them how adorable we are, they'll want to keep the family together.

 If I break my leg playing football, they'll have to both visit me in hospital.

If these types of thoughts sound familiar, you are not alone. These are the sort of things we all think when faced with a situation we don't want to accept. Our brain detects a problem and it comes up with a list of solutions, and some of the solutions can be pretty wild (like breaking a leg. Err ... Thanks, brain. Maybe not!)

Psychologists, who study the mind and our behaviour, have a special word for when our brain can't process what is happening. Denial. Unfortunately, although this denial might comfort us for a while, it is not the truth. Once your parents have decided to divorce or separate it is highly unlikely that they will get back together. Even though it's very hard, even though you may think they're wrong or acting childishly, they have made their decision and that can't be changed by anyone else.

Remember: They are still your parents – they are separating from one another, not from you. They will still love you just the same.

Thinking Differently

What if you made your family all go out on a boat for your birthday treat but then you got swept away to a desert island and your parents were stuck together and HAD to get on? That might work, right? Wrong. You know deep down what would happen. They would just get on each other's nerves and end up having more rows and everyone would still be unhappy, except now you'd be unhappy stuck on an island with only fish and coconuts to eat.

You can't stop your brain having a little daydream now and then, just to try to make you feel better, but eventually you will need to move on to accept the new situation. Your parents don't love each other like they used to, and there's nothing you can do to change that. What you can do instead, is accept that fact and start planning your new life.

Another important thing to accept is that it's not your fault. Nothing you did made your parents separate, even if they argued over you or involved you in their rows. Even if you got angry or behaved badly. None of it is about you. If you weren't there, they would have just found something else to disagree about.

Remember: It is not your fault they're divorcing. Just as you didn't break them up, you also can't get them back together. It's not your responsibility to make it better.

It Happened to Me

Gina's Story

When Gina's parents told her they were splitting up she desperately tried to think of ways to stop it.

My dad moved out to his own flat, it was horrible. I went to see him but it just felt all wrong and I was so upset that he'd bought some new coffee mugs because they were 'his' not 'our family's'. I got this crazy idea that if I caught some sort of mystery illness, he'd have come back to look after me. I even started going out without my coat on to try to get sick! But in the end I had a long talk with him and I realised that it wouldn't matter if I went to another planet and caught alien space flu – my parents just didn't love each other any more. They were splitting up whatever. Once I accepted this, things weirdly got a bit better. I stopped spending so much time stressing about it and started to think about what positive things I could do, like asking my dad if we could decorate my room at his flat. I still wish they were together and I still have sad days, but some things you just can't change. And my room is really cool!

Once our brains stop trying to find ways of wriggling out of the situation and realise we don't have any option but to go along with what our parents have decided, it can be a relief, but it can also leave us feeling very sad. Although it might not seem like it at the time, this sadness is a good thing. It shows we are accepting the situation, and once we do that we can move on to finding ways of managing our lives and feelings.

If you find yourself feeling very sad, that's a sign you need to take care of yourself. Remember, you and your poor brain have had a big shock. You need a bit of looking after. Maybe you have someone you can talk to – this is the time when a lovely, kind granny is useful to have around. But if you don't have a granny or someone similar to talk to, don't forget you can still talk to yourself in the same way.

Really, when you think about it, you are doing a great job. You have an awful lot of emotions to manage and changes to come to terms with, and you are getting on with things in a very mature way. But often we are more mean to ourselves than we would ever be to others. You need to remind yourself how well you're doing (psychologists call this 'self-talk'). If you find it difficult to know what to say to yourself, imagine your best friend was feeling like you do. What would you say to them?

 'You are doing so well. You are managing a very difficult situation brilliantly.'

 'Don't worry. Everything will work out in the end. You'll see.'

 'It's really tough right now, but you have lots of people who care for you and are there to help you.'

Write these phrases out in a little note to yourself. Keep it with you and read it when times get tough. Channel your own best friend!

Looking after yourself is not just about saying kind words – you can look after yourself in other ways too. If your parents are arguing a lot and that upsets you, find ways to remove yourself from the situation. Go for a walk (make sure your parents know where you're going), see a friend, sit at the end of the garden or listen to your favourite music through headphones.

DEALING WITH THE FEELING

Feeling down

The Cheer-Up List

What are the things that always make you feel better? A hot chocolate with squirty cream and marshmallows? Riding your bike? Baking a cake? Cuddling the dog? Watching *Paddington 2*? Playing Football Manager? Painting a picture? Dancing around your bedroom? Reading a book? Going for a run? Chatting with your friends? Listening to music?

Everyone's different, so make a list, draw a picture or make a collage of the things that cheer *you* up. Try to do at least one of these every day. These 'self-soothing' behaviours are fantastic skills to learn, as you will be able to use them for the rest of your life!

Even the worst situations have some good things come out of them. It may be hard to spot them at the moment but there will be some, and there will be more as time goes on. It's easy to get stuck in a 'This is a disaster!' frame of mind, but take a step back and have a rethink. There are always some positives. For example, there will probably be fewer arguments at home once your parents have their own space. Also, it's better to have happy parents who live apart than sad parents who live together. Although you may not see as much of the parent you're not living with, the time you do spend together may well be more fun, with fewer distractions.

Grab a Pen!

Make a list of the positive things that might come out of the separation. Keep adding to it as you find new things. **And bear these two things in mind:** Sometimes a positive is something not happening, like your parents not arguing so much. Sometimes a positive is something new happening, like having more time to chat to one parent alone, maybe because you go out for tea every week now.

Do you know someone else who's been in a similar situation? Ask them what positive things happened in their family. You might be surprised.

Well done. You have taken the first step and set out on your journey. At times over the coming months it might seem as if there is still a mountain in front of you but, like all adventurers, if you just focus on the next step and keep going, you will eventually get to the top of the mountain.

Survival Kit Essentials

1. ACCEPTANCE. Try to find a way to accept the situation rather than fight it.

2. POSITIVE SELF-TALK. Remind yourself, 'I am doing so well!'

3. SELF-CARE. Look after yourself and be kind to yourself. Make a 'cheer-up' list.

4. FIND THE POSITIVES. For you and your parents.

SAY IT OUT LOUD!

'I know this is a big change but I'm up to the challenge!'

'I'm going to find the positives, make sure I take good care of myself and start the journey into my new life.'

CHAPTER TWO

EMOTIONAL STORMS
HOW TO LEARN TO RECOGNISE YOUR FEELINGS AND DEAL WITH ANGER

'I'm not afraid of storms
for I'm learning how to sail
my ship.'

Amy, *Little Women*

Everyone who goes through a big life experience feels stronger-than-usual emotions. That's why people cry at weddings and cheer and shout when their team wins the League Championship. At least those situations are familiar, so we know what feelings to expect, but faced with a major upset like a parental separation, our brains can go into a bit of a flap and start flinging about all sorts of weird feelings. Here are some things you might feel:

Sad   Embarrassed   Scared

Angry   Happy   Ignored

Sulky   Childish   Exhausted

Hurt   Lonely   Irritable

Guilty

Giggly   Helpless

Excited   Anxious

Numb   Confused

Although this sounds like a list of Snow White's latest helpers, it's no fun if all these emotions are swirling around in your head. You might find you feel several of these things in a short space of time: angry one minute, giggly the next, then desperately sad and in need of a cuddle. These waves of feelings are perfectly natural. Just as you would eat a burger in lots of bites rather than one huge gulp, your brain can only process the situation in small chunks. This means there are lots of emotional ups and downs as each bit is worked through, and that can make it seem like you're being tossed around on a stormy sea.

DEALING WITH THE FEELING

Mixed up and confused

Look at the list of feelings on page 25. Write down which of these feelings you have experienced over the last week. Isn't it amazing how many feelings we have every day?

You can become your own feelings detective. Try to name your feelings as accurately as you can. So instead of thinking, 'I feel a bit meh,' it might be more true to think, 'I'm feeling sad and angry.'

The more you get to know and name your feelings, the more you feel just that little bit more in control of them.

Think about how long each feeling lasted. Most feelings don't last for long at any one time. Even if you are feeling really low, remember that this feeling will pass.

Remember: Feelings are like waves – they come and go. Some waves are big and noisy, others are smaller and more tickly. All day long we have waves of feelings, but they come and then they go.

Feelings are not just in our heads – how we are feeling can affect our entire bodies. For example, if you're really worrying about something, it might give you a pain in your tummy or make your head ache. If you're scared, your heart will beat faster and you might feel shaky. When we're sad we often feel heavy, like we have a wet towel on our shoulders.

Working out where and how we experience a feeling in our bodies can help us identify our feelings better, which then means we can manage them more easily.

Grab a Pen!

How are you feeling at the moment?

Draw an outline of yourself and label where in your body you feel different emotions. Think especially about your head, neck, chest and tummy. Shaky, sweaty hands and wobbly, weak knees are often good clues too. Don't worry about it being right or wrong, or different from other people's feelings – this is all about you.

Once we are able to recognise our feelings better, we can begin to learn how to deal with them. This also means they're less likely to explode out when we least expect them. Different feelings require different responses. Some feelings are easier to manage than others. If we're feeling irritable, maybe a few deep breaths and a bit of space will make us feel better, but some feelings are BIG. So big they can take you by surprise, knock you off balance and even make you scared.

TRY THIS

What emotion are you feeling now?
How strong is that emotion?

Rate it out of 10 on our special Emotion-o-meter.

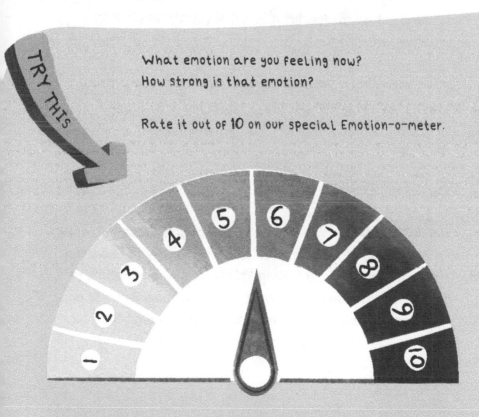

(You can copy the Emotion-o-meter into your journal.)

Try this exercise on different days and at different times – you will see that your emotions are not just on or off, sometimes they feel strong and sometimes not so much. The same situation can even give us different feelings at different times. (Although everyone feels sad when E.T. goes home.) Maybe you will see patterns in your feelings – such as feeling sad after leaving Mum's or feeling worried on a Thursday because it's PE at school.

Understanding these changes helps us to deal with the waves of emotions we have.

If you are feeling strong emotions, you will find ideas throughout the book to help you manage them.

Remember: We can't control the people around us, or all the things which happen to us, but we can learn to control our own thinking and feeling. This takes a whole lifetime to perfect, but you can start now by getting to know your feelings, understand why you're having them, and learning tools to help you manage these feelings.

One emotion that can feel difficult to manage is anger.

It Happened to Me

Kwame's Story

Kwame hated that he felt so angry inside all the time.

I couldn't really understand why but I just felt furious with everyone – my parents, my little sister, my friends, my teacher. It was like I had a volcano inside me just waiting to explode. I was always the happy one who made everyone laugh but now I was kind of scared at how I felt. One day I lost it in school and shouted at my teacher, knocked my chair over and ran out of class. I thought I was going to be in massive trouble, but my teacher was really good. When I calmed down, we had a long talk about how I was feeling. He helped me to talk to my parents, and now lets me have time out of class if everything is getting too much. At home I've started to do a lot of drawing and sketching, I really like it and it calms me down when my head is racing. If I notice my body is starting to get tense, I go on the trampoline. I know what to do with the anger a bit more. Now that everyone is talking about stuff I feel a lot happier.

There's nothing wrong with feeling angry. It's a natural reaction to unfairness or things being out of our control. A little bit of anger empowers us to stop something bad happening. For example, if you're in the park with your little brother and a bigger kid pushes him over, you feel angry because he can't defend himself, so you step in to protect him. Anger is your brain's way of saying, 'Hang on a minute. That's not right!'

When we get angry, we don't think things through as clearly as we normally would. That's why, if you feel angry, you suddenly get the courage to stand up to someone mean, when you've always been scared of them before.

But because anger stops us from thinking clearly, we have to be careful how we manage it, so it doesn't cause problems. If we let angry feelings get out of hand, they can take over and control our behaviour like an alien in a scary movie! For example, it's normal to feel angry if your sister breaks the Lego model you've been working on all week. However, it's not acceptable to hit or hurt her or to break something of hers in revenge. This just makes the situation worse and will probably end up with you feeling guilty and sad too.

Instead, you can use words to let her know how you are feeling: 'I feel really angry because I spent so much time on that model, and now it's all ruined.'

Your sister can then at least understand your feelings and might even help make it better (even if she can't rebuild it, she might at least help you pick up the pieces).

> **Remember:** Feeling angry is OK. It's what we do with that anger which can be a problem.

At times of change we are more likely to feel anger, because things are happening out of our control. If you find yourself feeling angry a lot, these are things you can try to stop the angry alien from taking over.

DEALING WITH THE FEELING
Anger

✳ REMOVE YOURSELF FROM THE SITUATION. Strong anger is a very short-lived emotion. If you can take yourself away from the person or situation you are angry with for just a few moments, you will probably find your anger fades. Walk into another room or outside.

✳ CONCENTRATE ON YOUR BREATHING. When we get angry, our breathing becomes very quick and shallow. We need to reverse this by breathing in nice, big, slow breaths. This sends a signal to our brain that it doesn't need to fire off angry alarms. Try some 'square breathing'.

First, draw a large square on a piece of paper. Put your finger on the top-left corner of the square, then slowly move it across to the other corner while you breathe in.

Pause when you get to the corner. Now follow the line down, slowly breathing out. You can do this going around the square a few times until you feel calmer. If you practise a few times you won't need the square – you can just imagine it.

* **TAKE IT OUT ON SOMETHING ELSE.** Kicking a football, bouncing on a trampoline or punching a cushion can help to use up the angry energy. Make sure it's something that can't be hurt or get broken, though.

* **FIND A SAFE PLACE TO SHOUT LOUDLY.** Shouting, stomping your feet, running or singing into the air can also get rid of the built-up energy. Just don't do it in the supermarket.

* **WRITE ALL OF YOUR FEELINGS DOWN IN AN ANGRY LETTER** – then tear it into tiny pieces and throw them away.

* **DRAW A PICTURE OF YOUR ANGER AS A PERSON.** Then add on a silly moustache, big bushy eyebrows, a spotty hat or whatever you want to make it less frightening.

* **PRACTISE THE WORDS YOU WANT TO SAY.** Strangely, anger has a way of taking away our words. Instead of being able to explain what's wrong we can find ourselves huffing and spluttering and shouting. Think about what has made you feel angry and practise how you will explain that feeling if it happens again. For example: 'I feel angry when you don't tell me what's going on,' or 'I feel angry now, and my body

feels like a volcano about to erupt.' or 'I need to go and stand outside until I feel calmer.' If you have a few well-rehearsed lines up your sleeve, it will be easier to express how you feel in the heat of the moment and people are more likely to understand and help.

* GIVE IT TIME. Once we've been angry in the day, it can take our body a few hours to calm all the way back down. If something else annoys you again before your body has calmed all the way down, it can lead to another surge of anger. This can make it 'one of those days' where you leap from one angry moment to another. On days like that, it is so important to look after yourself and calm your poor, overworked brain down.

Remember: If you feel your anger, sadness or other emotions are getting too big/strong for you to cope with, talk to someone. No one should ever feel they have to manage alone. Speak to your parents, or someone else you trust, and ask them to help you. It takes teamwork to get through a time like this.

Being the child of a family going through a divorce or separation means you grow up fast. No matter how much your parents try to protect you from what's happening you will hear and see things that a lot of other kids don't.

They may be arguing a lot, shouting, or just not speaking to each other. You might see them upset or crying. They may be short-tempered with you, or sometimes seem as if they've forgotten you exist altogether. This may make you feel angry with your parents, but try to remember they are going through a tough time too. They really did intend to stay together forever and now they are having to find a new way forward. They will be emotional and stressed, and this can cause people to act in unexpected ways.

Understanding this can help you see that they are just not being themselves at the moment, and although that might be annoying or make you anxious, if everyone in the family supports each other, it will pass, and things will settle down.

Thinking Differently

Training your brain

When we're angry with someone it's hard to see the nice or good things about them. Instead our brains tend to just focus on the things they do or say that carry on making us angry. But there are lots of positive things about that person as well. Train your brain to focus on these by reminding yourself of some of the good things. Complete these sentences:

✳ One thing I like about .... is ....
✳ One happy memory I have with them is when ....
✳ I am grateful to them for...................
✳ In the future I hope that............... and I will be able to

Remember: If you are scared about someone becoming so angry they use violence against either you or someone else (hitting, punching or otherwise hurting), then you need to talk to someone about it. Speak to an adult you trust, or contact an organisation such as Childline who can help and advise you. Contact details are at the back of the book.

Survival Kit Essentials

1. NAME THE FEELING. Try to find the right words for what you feel.

2. LOCATE THE FEELING. Recognise where you feel it in your body.

3. TRACK YOUR FEELINGS. In a journal or on a chart. Use pictures or words, whatever works best for you. You will then start to find patterns in how you feel.

4. MANAGE YOUR ANGER. This can feel like a big, scary emotion, but it can be understood and managed, just like every other emotion.

5. LOOK FOR THE POSITIVES. Don't let anger cloud your judgement of others.

SAY IT OUT LOUD!

'It's completely natural to
have these strong feelings, so I
don't need to be frightened of them. I know
they will come and go, but by learning about
them I will understand myself even more.'

CHAPTER THREE

FINDING YOUR ANCHOR
HOW TO MANAGE YOUR ANXIETIES AND GAIN A SENSE OF CONTROL

'You can't change conditions. Just the way you DEAL with them.'

Jessica Watson OAM, sailor

Sometimes, when big life changes happen, we have days when we feel that everything is such a muddle we'll never get our lives back together. One thing changing, such as our parents separating, means another thing changes, like maybe where we live, and before we know it everything seems to be changing and there's nothing we can do about it. This can leave us feeling like we're all at sea, in a small boat, with no oars and no anchor. Argh! This is especially difficult for young people as they have much less control over what's happening than the adults involved. It can seem like you have unpleasant surprises sprung on you all the time and you're just waiting to find out what the next one is going to be.

TRY THIS

If you're feeling like you're in a little boat being tossed around on a rough sea, try these two exercises to help you feel more 'anchored'.

Grounding Exercise

Sit in a chair or on a stool with your feet on the floor. Push your feet into the floor and notice how you can feel the solid ground underneath. Push your bottom into the chair.

Notice how you can feel the chair underneath you. Feel how the chair and the ground are completely supporting you.

Take some big, slow breaths.

The 3, 2, 1 Exercise

Next look around and notice:

✳ 3 things you can see
✳ 2 things you can hear
✳ 1 thing you can smell

Take some big, slow breaths. How do you feel? More relaxed?

These are exercises in mindfulness (maybe you've done some mindfulness at school). They are designed to help you focus on the here and now, and this stops your brain from whizzing off to worry about the future, or flying back to fret about the past.

Thinking like this acts like an anchor in the present and helps your body and brain to realise that it is safe, right here, right now. You can do these exercises any time you feel tense or worried, wherever you are – at school, on a bus, even when you're having your tea – and no one else will notice (unless you get so relaxed you fall asleep in the spaghetti).

Exercises like this are things we can do inside our heads to help keep us feeling calm; we call them 'internal anchors'. But there are 'external anchors' too. These can be dependable people or activities which make us feel comfortable and secure. Your anchors might be your weekly football practice, a cuddle with your dog, a Thursday afternoon dance class, your favourite auntie who drops in every week and always brings you a cake, or simply your favourite TV programme. These things remind us that life is still reliably ticking along – they are like a solid anchor in a stormy sea.

Grab a Pen!

Think about your external anchors. What are the reliable things in your life which make you feel secure? Write them into this anchor, or copy it into your journal.

Once you know what your anchors are, you can work hard to keep them in your life. Let your parents know what your anchors are so they can prioritise them even with all of the changes your family is going through.

COPING WITH CHANGES

Everything in life changes. The seasons change, the weather changes, the school lunch menu changes – sometimes you even change your socks. (You do, right?)

Most of the time this is a good thing. It's what makes life an adventure! It would be very boring if everything stayed the same. If the cinema always showed the same movie and you always had the same dinner and every day it rained. Not many of us would want that.

Barack Obama, the former President of the United States, says his mum told him, 'The world is complicated, Bar. That's why it's interesting.'

Still, it's only natural to be a little concerned about things changing. Our brains are programmed to think about possible problems and work out ways to head them off in advance. An explorer setting off on an expedition thinks about the weather and how it might change, the possibility of getting sick or the path being blocked. They make sure they take protective clothing, first-aid supplies and the right tools. If they sauntered into the jungle in a pair of flip-flops and a swimming costume they wouldn't last long! So, thinking about possible dangers ahead and making some plans to tackle them is a sensible and organised way to go about our lives. But allowing our thoughtful planning to turn into uncontrolled worry and anxiety is not, and this is what we have to watch out for.

It's very easy to get caught up in worries about the future when your parents are separating. There may be a lot of uncertainty about where you are going to live, which school you will go to and how you will stay in touch with your relatives. Our brains can get hung up on trying to think of every possible way to manage the situation and that's when we get anxious.

Thinking Differently

Take a minute to try to remember what you were worrying about this time last year. Or the year before. Chances are you can't remember, and all that worry was, well, a bit of a waste of time. Even if you can remember – all the worrying didn't change the way things happened. Worrying is like sitting on a swing – it gives you something to do but doesn't get you anywhere!

Remember: Things could go wrong, but they could also just as well go right. Worrying about it won't make the outcome any different.

Our brains are excellent at imagining. In fact, they are so good they often can't really tell the difference between what's real and what's not. For example, think of your favourite food, cooked just how you like it. Think of the smell, the taste and the way it feels in your mouth. Now imagine you have a big steamy forkful and you are about to take a delicious bite.

45

Mmmm! You will probably find your mouth is already watering in readiness for the food it is about to eat. You may start feeling hungry – your stomach might even rumble! Even though the food is completely imaginary, your brain is sending your body signals that it's going to get a lovely dinner, just because you imagined it! If you are feeling stressed or tense you can also use this imagination superpower to help you relax.

Find a quiet place where you won't be disturbed and close your eyes.

Now think of a calm place, maybe a peaceful beach. Imagine lying on a comfy sun-lounger. Listen to the sound of the waves gently swooshing over the sand. Feel the warm sun on your skin and a gentle breeze ruffling your hair. Take a deep breath, and really smell the sea air. Relax. Your body will act as if it really is there on the beach, relaxed and calm.

Your special place doesn't have to be a beach – it can be wherever you want it to be, whatever makes you feel relaxed, just make sure to feel, hear and smell what's around you. You can visit your calm place whenever you need to just by taking a few moments to imagine yourself there. The more you practise this, the better at it you will become, and you will soon be able to relax whenever you want to!

I NEED CONTROL!

One way our brains sometimes deal with feeling
uncertain is to try to control things around us.
For example, by cleaning, tidying and
organising things. Perhaps you've noticed
you always get an uncontrollable
urge to reorganise your
pencil case when you're
supposed to be revising
for a test. Even superstar
footballer David Beckham
used to tidy his hotel room
before playing a match.

It's useful to learn to spot these behaviours. If you
find yourself arranging your socks in order of the colours of the rainbow
it might be because you feel something else is not in your control (although
it might also look very nice).

There's nothing wrong with routines like this if they make you feel happier
and calmer, but if you start to worry when you don't do them, or they start
taking up too much of your time, then that's just giving yourself another
reason to feel anxious and adding to the problem.

It Happened to Me

Aaliyah's Story
Aaliyah felt her world was spinning out of control.

When my parents split up I felt so scared and unhappy. I kept thinking if that could happen then something else bad might happen. It was as if there were no rules about life any more. I don't really know why but I kept thinking if I kept my room tidy then at least that bit of my life was not a mess. It was OK at first, Mum was super-pleased! But then I started to worry if anything was out of place, I kept thinking if I didn't line my shoes up or pick my clothes up something would go wrong. It was getting so I had to keep going back to check my room before I left the house. Mum started to realise that it was taking me longer and longer to get ready in the morning because I had to tidy my room first. We had a long talk and she said she understood how I was feeling but I was letting it affect me too much. I ended up meeting with a counsellor who helped me to learn to relax and also made me realise that there was no connection with how tidy my room was and what happened in life. We just can't control everything. Now I still like to keep things organised but I'm not so worried about it. Me and Mum also know to keep an eye out in case I start feeling stressed like that again.

In the end, there's only one thing to say about controlling the future. We can't. No one can, not celebrities or scientists or presidents. This is something we just have to accept. Worrying about things we can't predict or change just makes us unhappy today – and it doesn't change a thing about tomorrow. We can't stop things changing and we can't control what other people do. But we can control what we focus on and take positive actions to make ourselves feel better.

Grab a Pen!

Our brains are designed to notice things that are different – it's one of the things that help keep us safe. If you didn't notice a broken paving stone you might trip and get hurt. So far, so helpful – thanks, brain. However, a big change in our life, like our parents separating, can make our brain forget to notice that many things are still the same. It goes into 'Operation High Alert!' and thinks it's doing us a favour by pointing out EVERYTHING that has changed. This can leave us feeling super-confused and lost and wobbly. So, you need to give your brain a helping hand. Have two pieces of paper. One headed 'Things that are different' and one headed 'Things that are the same as always'.

Write or draw on each paper what is different. For example:

✳ I have two bedrooms
✳ Dad has a new car
✳ There's a new girl in my class

And what is the same:

* Both bedrooms are still really messy
* Mum still goes on about homework more than Dad
* Wednesday is pizza for lunch

When you feel as if you are being tossed about in a whirlpool, confused and unsure, keep reading your 'Things that are the same as always' list. This will encourage and remind your brain to also pay attention to what is the same.

WORRY, WORRY, WORRY!

This is bound to be a worrying time, and it would a bit strange if you didn't have some concerns about what the future holds. (But if you don't – great stuff. You are officially super-chilled!) Our brain likes it when everything is predictable – even soggy school pizza on a Wednesday. When things are predictable we can run on auto-pilot. Our brain doesn't have to think about much, and it can rest. The kind of brain equivalent of swinging in a hammock sipping a banana-and-pineapple smoothie. But when things don't go to plan and there's a big change, suddenly it's all action stations. Captain Brain leaps out of the hammock, throws the smoothie in the hedge and goes into hyper-drive, looking out for all the things that are different and sending your body signals that it needs to 'Prepare for action!'

Now this sort of reaction might have been very useful in prehistoric times when danger from wild animals, reptiles, insects and other tribe members

was an everyday event, but – unless you're a contestant on *I'm a Celebrity, Get Me Out of Here* – it's probably a bit over the top for modern life.

Of course, there are still dangers we face every day. When we cross the road we are on high alert for vehicles, listening closely and being very aware of sudden movements, but we don't need to be like this all the time. Unfortunately, our brains haven't really caught up with the modern age, and they can start sending out 'Prepare for action!' alarms for all sorts of reasons which aren't life-and-death situations at all.

Knowing your parents are separating can set off those signals. The problem is, as we saw earlier, there are just some things we can't know or predict, and if our thoughts keep looping around, trying to find answers, our brain just can't relax. It spends all day scanning for danger and checking out other people and even wakes us up to worry in the night. So you wake up, heart racing, feeling exhausted before the day has even started. Walking around you notice all the other kids looking happy, all the other parents holding hands and smiling at each other, you become an expert on your teachers' facial expressions, noticing whether they're cross or excited or happy. Your brain is in survival mode. It's realised things aren't how they used to be so it's going to stay awake 24 hours a day making sure it's protecting you.

Thanks, brain! This is what anxiety is. A shaky, stressy, wobbly feeling and thoughts about all the bad things that are going to happen and how there is no way you are going to be able to cope with it. Wrong. You can and you will cope with it. You just need to work your way through this time of change, step by step.

DEALING WITH THE FEELING

Anxiety

Make a list of things that you are worrying about right now. Now draw three columns in your journal and head them: 'I can change this'; 'I can change some of this'; and 'I can't change this'. Look at your worries and put them into each column. For example: 'I'll get in trouble if I don't do my maths homework' can definitely go into column 1. 'I might not get to see my grandad this weekend' can go into column 2. 'Lewis Hamilton might not win on Sunday' would go into column 3.

I can change this

These are the things to focus your energy on and get the 'quick wins' under your belt. You can do your homework – you might not want to, but you can. Problem solved. Do the work, give yourself a big high-five and put a line through that problem.

I can change some of this

Write out two or three things you can do that would help with each problem. Think creatively. You might not be able to get exactly what you want, but perhaps you could do it in a different way. For example, if you can't see your grandad as often as you'd like, maybe you can chat to him online – or send a letter. If your parents don't want to come to the school play together, maybe they can come on separate evenings.

I can't change this

Finally, whatever Column 3s are left you're just simply going to have to stop worrying about. There are some things in life that we just can't control (and Lewis Hamilton will understand).

If you are still feeling 'all at sea', it may be that your parents haven't been explaining things to you very well. This isn't because they don't think you or your feelings are important, but they are probably a bit distracted by everything that's going on. Parents often don't realise how worried children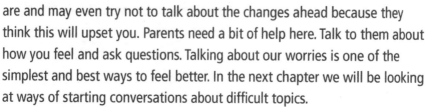

are and may even try not to talk about the changes ahead because they think this will upset you. Parents need a bit of help here. Talk to them about how you feel and ask questions. Talking about our worries is one of the simplest and best ways to feel better. In the next chapter we will be looking at ways of starting conversations about difficult topics.

Survival Kit Essentials

1.   KEEP CALM AND CARRY ON! Use grounding and take big, slow breaths.

2.   IDENTIFY YOUR EXTERNAL ANCHORS. Try to keep them in your life.

3.   USE YOUR IMAGINATION. Try finding your own special, calm, imaginary place to help you feel relaxed.

4.   TRAIN YOUR BRAIN. Notice what is the same as well as what is different.

5.   WORK OUT WHAT YOU CAN AND CAN'T CHANGE. Focus your energy on the things you can change.

6.   TALK IT OUT. Talking is one of the simplest ways to feel better fast.

7.   BE AWARE OF YOUR WORRYING BRAIN. Just because you feel worried, that doesn't mean something bad is going to happen. Things could just as easily turn out fine.

SAY IT OUT LOUD!

'I know there are some things in my life I can't control, so I won't let them stress me!'

'I will concentrate on what I can control, like my thoughts and responses, and that will make me feel a lot better.'

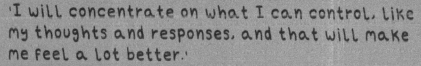

CHAPTER FOUR

NAVIGATING THE WAY
HOW TO FIND OUT WHAT YOU NEED TO KNOW AND EXPLAIN HOW YOU FEEL

'Come on. Group hug.
You too, ANGER.'

Joy, *Inside Out*

When you find out your parents are splitting up you will have a lot of things you are unsure of and questions you want answers to. Questions like 'Where will I live?' and 'When will I see the parent I'm not living with?' are some of the most obvious ones, but there will be many more. Unfortunately, parents aren't always in the mood to answer questions. Perhaps some of these sound familiar:

Most young people will recognise these phrases. Even the most patient parent can be distracted by other things going on during day-to-day life and brush you off when you're trying to get some answers. Normally, if you're just asking something like 'Is my PE top washed?' not getting an answer can be annoying but not very important. But if your parents are splitting up you will have a lot more important things you want to find out about and if your parents aren't really listening it can be frustrating and worrying. You might even start to feel they don't care about you or how you feel.

But hold on, they're having to deal with lots of changes right now too. Your parents really do want the best outcome for the family and they will be working hard to get things organised. They will both have a lot of difficult emotions to manage themselves and, at the same time, a lot of practical stuff to sort out like money, housing and legal matters. Unfortunately, our brains can only work on one difficult thing at a time. When we try to think about a lot of different things at once our brain has trouble coping.

TRY THIS

Grab your pen and write out the words to your favourite song.

Hold on!
At the same time, count backwards from 100 out loud.

Hold on!
At the same time, twirl your right foot anticlockwise.

How did you get on? Tough, eh?

If you feel like your parents are not giving you as much attention as usual this could be why – they just have too much on their plate to do all at once. No wonder they're a bit stressed and distracted. Be patient and remember they won't always be like this.

In the meantime, try working on this Three-Step Communication Plan.

THE THREE-STEP COMMUNICATION PLAN

Step One: All the questions

In your journal, make a list of things you want to know about. Here are some questions which might be important to you.

* Where will I live?
* Do we have to leave our house?
* Who will I live with?
* When will I see each parent?
* Can I still see my grandparents?
* Do I have to change school?
* Who will pick me up from school?
* Who will look after the pets?
* Where will I go for big family celebrations (Christmas/Diwali/Hanukkah/Eid etc.)
* What will happen in the school holidays?
* Where will I go for my birthday?

There might be lots of other things you think of too. No question is a silly question if it's bothering you. Write them all down in your notebook and add to it as more things occur to you. Writing things down is a great tip for any worries; it gets stuff out of your head and frees up your brain space.

As well as questions there may be other things you want to say too. Perhaps you have feelings you want to talk about or some things you want to stop happening. Whatever it is, make sure you write it down until you can find the right time to talk.

Look at your questions and work out who the best person is to ask. Write that person's name (there might be more than one) next to the question. Some questions may be more important to you than others. Put a number 1 by the most important thing you want to ask, number 2 by the next and so on. This will help you to organise your thoughts and make sure you get answers to the most pressing questions if you run out of time.

Once you have all your thoughts organised, you're ready for ...

Step Two: Find the right time

Choose a time when the person you want to speak to is not too busy. It's no good trying to talk to a parent if they are rushing around in the morning, busy getting the dinner ready or in the middle of watching their favourite sport or TV show. Often the best thing to do is to ask them straight out, 'Can I have a bit of quiet time to talk to you soon?' Make an appointment like you would do if you were a businessperson. After all, this is important stuff. If your mum says something like 'OK, after school, tomorrow,' remind her again before school. Parents have a habit of forgetting things when they are

busy. If your appointment does get 'cancelled' because someone forgot or was unexpectedly busy, don't be cross or give up – just get them to agree another time. Eventually they will give you the time you need.

Now it's time for ...

Step Three: Talking things through

For this sort of chat, it's probably best to sit somewhere quiet. If this isn't possible at home then going out for a walk or to a coffee shop might work too, but remember to bring your book with you. When everything is quiet and calm, take a deep breath and begin.

Even when you have all your notes and you've made the right time, it's not always easy to find the right way to say things. For example, if you're discussing something like who you'd prefer to live with, you might worry that what you say you will upset the parent you're speaking with. But some things have to be discussed even if they are upsetting, so be brave and remember, your parents are adults and are probably expecting these questions anyway.

Once you've said what you want to say, it's time to let the other person speak. Communication is about listening as well as talking. Even if you don't agree with what's being said, or you feel they haven't really understood, try not to argue or interrupt until they have finished their point. Then it's your turn to say what you think again. Doing it this way means there's less chance of an argument breaking out and someone ending the chat by getting cross or walking out. Work your way through your notes and if you don't have time to get to the end, ask if you can have another chat in a few days' time.

It Happened to Me

Mo's Story

When Mo's parents split up he had so many questions but didn't know how to ask them.

My dad moved out, so I was only seeing him at weekends. I didn't feel like I could ask him stuff because he just wanted to do fun stuff like play on the Xbox together and go for a run in the park. It never seemed to be the right time to talk about serious things and I didn't want to make him feel bad, but I'd overheard him telling his mate that he might go to work abroad and I was really worried. In the end I just took a deep breath and blurted it out right in the middle of a game of FIFA. He was so surprised he let in a goal! But then we paused the game and had a proper talk. He said he might have to go to Germany for a week with work but that was all. He said he would never move so far that we couldn't spend weekends together. He said he was glad we'd talked and now he often asks me if there's anything I want to chat about.

Another thing to consider is that you might not get answers to everything you want to know straight away. Your parents might not know the answers themselves yet. When it comes to big issues around homes and schools, there is a lot of discussion and negotiation that goes on; everybody wants to be sure to make the right choices. Your parents will probably have to speak to a solicitor at some point (a solicitor is someone who deals with legal matters). There may even be some questions that have to be decided by a judge in a 'family court'. This doesn't mean that anyone has done anything wrong. A family court is very different to a criminal court. A judge in a family court helps make decisions about the best living arrangements for children if their parents just can't agree, and no one gets in trouble.

As you can see, there is a lot that needs to be worked through. Try to be patient. Keep putting things in your journal and use the relaxation ideas in Chapter Three to help you if you're feeling worried.

Thinking Differently

It can be difficult to relax when we don't know all the answers. Our brain will try to fill in the gaps with all sorts of imaginings about what might happen – and it nearly always seems to come up with worrying ideas. This is one of those times when our brain is trying to be helpful but failing rather badly. We have these negative thoughts so we can think about what to do in a worst case and help prepare for it, but that doesn't mean it's going to happen. It can be helpful to remember that we don't have to believe everything we think, it's just our brain chattering away and that doesn't mean it's likely to happen.

DEALING WITH THE FEELING

Sadness

Although talking things through always helps in the long run, focusing on the situation can leave us feeling sad. This is a natural reaction. Something you loved has changed completely and you will miss the way things used to be. Sadness does get less as time passes and, although it's hard to see now, there will come a time when you are your old happy self once more.

In the meantime, let yourself feel sad when that wave comes along. Remind yourself that it's a natural reaction which shows you really do care about the things that have changed or been lost. Pay attention to it, look after yourself and get to know that, like a wave, it will pass and you can get back to your life again.

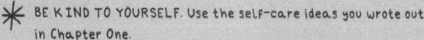

Ideas to try

✳ BE KIND TO YOURSELF. Use the self-care ideas you wrote out in Chapter One.

✳ HAVE A GREAT BIG CRY. Crying is the body's natural way of releasing bottled-up emotions. That's why we nearly always feel better after we've had a good cry. Never believe anyone who tells you that crying is babyish or that boys or big girls don't cry. Andy Murray, Lewis Hamilton, Beyoncé and Rihanna have all had a good cry on TV at different times – and it hasn't done them any harm.

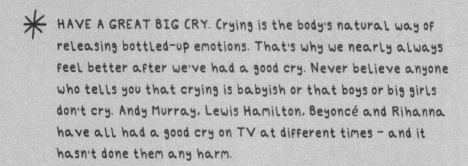

✳ TALK TO SOMEONE WHO CARES AND WILL LISTEN. Talking it out with a close friend, a caring teacher or one of your favourite relatives is one of the best ways to make yourself feel better.

✳ WRITE A JOURNAL. Just like talking, writing can get some of the sad stuff out of our heads and into the open. There is something about keeping stuff bottled up inside which always seems to make it feel worse, so get your scribble on.

✳ WATCH SOMETHING THAT MAKES YOU LAUGH. It's very hard to feel sad watching a skateboarding bulldog in a baseball cap.

TRY THIS

Put one of your hands on your heart as you sit down. Focus on your breathing and think of that hand as being full of love, and you are putting all of that love into your heart. Stay like this for a minute so that you can really feel all that care and love you are giving yourself. You will feel recharged and ready to take on anything after that!

Survival Kit Essentials

1. THREE-STEP COMMUNICATION PLAN. Communication is about listening as well as talking. Practise both with the Three-Step Plan.

2. BE PATIENT. Parents are very distracted at this time. You may need to work through your plan a few times with them before you get the information you need.

3. TALK TO OTHERS ABOUT YOUR FEELINGS. Just saying or writing the words can immediately make the feelings more manageable.

4. SELF-CARE. Be extra kind to yourself when you feel sad.

SAY IT OUT LOUD!

'I can learn to communicate clearly to get the answers I need and to explain my feelings.'

'I am a super-communicator! I know how to explain my feelings and get the answers I need.'

CHAPTER FIVE

A MOUNTAIN OF EMBARRASSMENT
HOW TO EXPLAIN THE SITUATION TO OTHERS AND GET SUPPORT

'Nobody should be ashamed. Everyone's situations are DIFFERENT, upbringings are DIFFERENT, communities are DIFFERENT.'

Marcus Rashford MBE, footballer

I f and when you tell other people that your parents are separating is your decision, although it's probably better to let your friends and teacher know what's going on sooner rather than later so they can understand and support you. Telling others may not be a big deal for you, you may be the sort of person who will just tell people at lunch and then just get on with your peanut-butter sandwich. That's great if it works for you. But for a lot of young people, having to tell others about their parents' separation can feel like another mountain to get over. A mountain of awkwardness, anxiety and embarrassment. If you feel that way you may have some thoughts like this:

What if people think my family's not normal? What if people ask me personal questions I don't know the answers to? What if other kids talk about me in the playground? What if my teacher gives me that 'you poor thing' look? What if some of my friends are mean about it? What if they think it's all my fault?

Yep. It's possible that some of those things will happen and, as we've seen already, there's not much we can do to control how other people react. But most people just want to help. Give them a chance and you will probably be surprised at how supportive and kind they are.

Thinking Differently

Look at this list. Which of these families do you think is normal?

* Marika lives with her mother and their dog.
* Yulia lives with her two dads in term time and with her mum in the holidays.
* Bao lives with his brother, mum and dad, and their three cats.
* Advik lives in a house with his twin baby sisters, his mum and his grandad.
* Gracie lives with her dad in the week and her mum and her girlfriend at the weekend.
* Qasim and Saad live with their aunt and uncle and their cousin.
* Hanna lives with her dad and step-mum and half-sister.
* Leandro lives with his adoptive father.
* Tyrone and Elise live with their mum and her friend, and her friend's daughter.

Answer: They all are – or maybe none of them are!
(Sorry – a bit of a trick question!)

There really is no such thing as a 'normal' family.

All of the people in the above examples consider themselves to be living with their family, and all of their situations are different. When people say 'normal' they really mean 'traditional', which usually translates as a mum and dad and children living together. This may have been the most common set-up in the past, but times have changed and many families are now non-traditional in one way or another. There are single-parent families; same-sex parent families; blended families (where some or all of the children are from the parents' previous relationships); adoptive

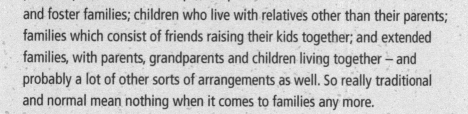

and foster families; children who live with relatives other than their parents; families which consist of friends raising their kids together; and extended families, with parents, grandparents and children living together – and probably a lot of other sorts of arrangements as well. So really traditional and normal mean nothing when it comes to families any more.

Who we choose to call our family is really up to us. We don't even have to be related. You can be in a family of two or a family of twenty. You can live in the same house or different houses. Some adults who live together consider themselves a family even though they don't have children. Family is not about being the same as everyone else. Family is about love and care and relationships. If they are your family, you know.

There is nothing to feel embarrassed about if your parents are separating. Be proud of your family, whatever form it takes.

My Family Tree

This is a fun way of looking at your family and all of the different relationships within it. Just like a tree, there can be lots of branches and leaves, but everyone is connected.

Draw a tree trunk and put your name on it. (Don't worry what it looks like, it's your own personal tree, it can look any way you like!) Now add a branch for each part of your family as it is now. Write the different people who live together on leaves. Don't forget to include grandparents, step-parents, aunties, cousins and pets. For example:

 Branch 1: Dad, Delia, Sammy the dog.
Branch 2: Uncle Jeff, Auntie Philly, Jess, Rosa, Jonson.

If some people move around you can have a leaf for them on more than one branch. Families are complicated, messy things but with you in the centre, can you see how important you are to that family?

INFORMATION CONTROL

When something big happens, such as our parents splitting up, we can feel very out of control of our lives. Things are happening to us which we can't do anything to stop. This is a deeply uncomfortable feeling and our brains try to help us feel better by finding something – anything – we can have control over. Sometimes, the thing we end up trying to control is the information we have about our lives, so we can become very particular about who we share this information with. It's like we put up a big fence and just want to keep everything to ourselves and not let other people in. But, as everyone knows, bottling things up like this is not good for our wellbeing. Talking things out with someone is one of the best ways of feeling better about problems. If we don't tell our friends what's happening it stops them being able to help and support us, and we risk feeling even more out of control! Phew! That all sounds like hard work. We need to give ourselves a break.

If you find yourself thinking like this, try to use your control, not to keep everything to yourself, but to figure out what you want to tell people. When people don't have access to all of the information, they fill the gaps with guesses. Sometimes these guesses might be right, but often they're wrong. Your friend might think you're being moody because of something they've done; your teacher might think you're not paying attention in class because you're being lazy.

Mind the Gap Story

Fill in the gaps in the story below. Then compare it with the version on page 158.

Once upon a time there was ....

But the .... was sad because

.... One day he/she/they met a ....

who was sad because ....

'Don't worry!' said the ....

'I can help you by ....'

The .... was so happy. 'And I can help you too!' he/she/they

said. 'Because ....'

And so they all lived........................ ever after.

Your story will be different because you had to fill in the gaps without knowing all the information. Ask someone else to try it and see what they come up with.

Giving people the essential information is a way of being in control. It's making sure the stuff they know is correct and means they won't start making up their own stories about you. In these ways you are still in control of what other people know, but you are making your life easier too.

Another reason we may not want to talk about our parents separating is because we don't want people to feel sorry for us, or to talk about us and our family. It can feel very awkward to be the centre of attention. As we grow towards our teenage years our brains naturally become super-sensitive to embarrassment. This is another one of those brain things left over from prehistoric times. Our cave-person ancestors needed to be accepted by their tribe for protection and safety so their natural instinct was to try to be the same as the other tribe members and not be seen as different. Part of our brain still worries about this sort of thing, so we still feel uncomfortable if we stand out from the crowd. But even though this is an understandable and natural feeling, we have to get past it and think about whether keeping things in is going to help or hinder us in the long run.

Remember: You have the right to keep things about your life private, but no one can help if they don't know what's going on. Letting go of information can be a scary thought, but when you do it, it can feel a great relief.

It Happened to Me

Bianca's Story

Bianca didn't know what to say when her friend asked why her dad didn't drop her off at school any more.

I didn't want to tell her it was because he'd moved out. I didn't even want to say it out loud because that would sort of make it real. So, I just said he'd got a new job. But then she asked me what his new job was, and I didn't know what to say. I blurted out, 'He's joined the police!'

I don't know why I said it. It was completely not true, but it was the first thing that came into my head. Then another friend asked me if he had a police car and a uniform – it was awful. I didn't want to keep lying but I didn't know what to say. That night I was so moody that my mum noticed and managed to get me to tell her what was wrong. She thought it was pretty funny actually, which I suppose it was in a way. My dad is a bus driver, I can't imagine him chasing criminals! She said I'd feel much better if I told them the truth. That night I decided to send a text to both of my friends. I just wrote:

'My parents are getting divorced and my dad has moved out, he's not in the police. I'm sorry I lied – I was just embarrassed. I don't really want everyone to know at the moment so I'm just telling you.'

My friends messaged me back saying nice things. The next day, they gave me a hug and one of them had baked me some 'cheer-up' cookies. Now it's much easier to talk to them about what's going on at home.

TELLING OTHERS

Think about who you want to tell and what is the most comfortable way of letting them know. For some people you will just want to give basic information in order for them to know what's going on for you. For example, you could simply say, 'My parents are splitting up,' or 'We are going through some family changes,' or 'I'm moving house,' and it will help them to understand. For closer friends who will look after you and support you, you will probably want to explain more.

✳ TALKING FACE TO FACE. This is often the best way of communicating as you can explain your feelings clearly and see the other person's reaction. This is the most direct way of communicating and so has the least potential for misunderstanding. It's also the only way if you want them to give you a hug afterwards! Use the Three-Step Communication Plan in Chapter Four to help you.

✳ BY MESSAGE OR TEXT, ETC. Sometimes it's easier to say things indirectly. This means you can work out what you want to say beforehand and people can get over their surprise and think about their reactions and feelings before responding.

✳ ASKING SOMEONE ELSE TO EXPLAIN WHAT'S GOING ON FOR YOU. This is a good idea if you just don't know how to start the conversation (more tips on that below). Your parents may have already spoken to your teacher, but if they haven't, and you don't feel comfortable doing it yourself, ask them to do so.

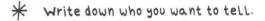

Grab a Pen!

* Write down who you want to tell.

* Think about the way you want to tell them.

* What will you say? Practise saying this out loud or write out your text.

WHAT TO DO IF SOMEONE ASKS YOU TOO MANY QUESTIONS

You don't have to answer any questions you don't want to. Most people will probably just be curious, but some questions can make you feel uncomfortable. Even your friends' parents can get very nosey and not consider your feelings. The easiest way to deal with this is just to shrug and say a quick 'I'm not sure'. If they are persistent or keep asking you, practise standing up tall, looking up and saying, 'I'd rather not talk about it.' You are not being rude, you are just stating how you feel.

WHAT TO DO IF SOMEONE IS MEAN

Unkind people are part of life. There are people who just like to get a 'reaction', so they will say something mean about your family or one of your parents to see if they can upset you or make you angry.

Sigh! Some people learn to play guitar. Some people bake great cakes. Some people play basketball. And some people can't come up with anything better to do than pick on someone else and try to hurt them. Really, we should feel sorry for them, because people who do this kind of thing are people who are unhappy and unsure of themselves. Do your best not to show them you're upset, take a big breath, turn away, walk away and be glad you have a more interesting life. If it gets to be a problem, speak to an adult you trust about what is happening.

Remember: If someone is bullying you, you do not have to put up with it alone. Ask your friends to help you out and speak to an adult you trust. There are also other places you can get advice and information, listed at the back of this book.

Telling other people about your family situation can feel uncomfortable at first. However, just like going to the dentist or having a jab, it's best to get it over with and move on with your life. You don't have to go into the playground with a loudhailer, but telling a few key friends when you feel the time is right will help them to understand and support you. You may even find they have been through something similar themselves and can give you good advice.

Survival Kit Essentials

1. ACCEPTANCE. Remember that your family is still your family and as normal as anyone else's.

2. OPEN UP. Talking about your parents' divorce might make you feel embarrassed at times but you have nothing to be ashamed of. This is not your fault.

3. REACH OUT. Think about the support you might have around you. You don't have to tell anyone anything you don't want to, but no one can help or support you if they don't know what's actually happening.

4. WRITE. Use your journal to work out who you want to tell and how you want to tell them. Use a Three-Step Communication Plan to help you.

5. BE HONEST. Tell the truth. It's much easier in the long run (you won't have to remember what you've made up for one thing).

6. TELL SCHOOL. Make sure your school knows the situation at home. Ask your parents for help in telling teachers.

SAY IT OUT LOUD!

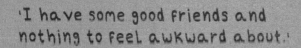

'I have some good friends and nothing to feel awkward about.'

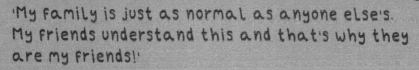

'My family is just as normal as anyone else's. My friends understand this and that's why they are my friends!'

CHAPTER SIX

CROSSWINDS
HOW TO MANAGE IF YOUR PARENTS PUT YOU IN THE MIDDLE

'You never REALLY understand a person until you consider things from his point of view.'

Atticus Finch, *To Kill a Mockingbird*

One thing that may dawn on you, when your parents split up, is that they are human. (Unless you are an alien, in which case, Greetings!)

When we are very young, we tend to think of our parents as a bit like superheroes. We think they can sort out any problem, that they always know best and always do the right thing. We believe what they tell us and trust them to make the right decisions. We think they are strong and clever and brave and make the best pancakes on the planet! Most people go on believing this about their parents for years. And parents do their best to live up to that expectation, they do try hard to be the best they can be. But of course, they are not superheroes, they are just humans, and humans are not perfect.

Children of parents who are splitting up often realise this much earlier than other kids. This is another one of those ways that going through a parental separation makes you deeply wise!

When we are going through a stressful time, it's not always easy to be our best selves. If we get full to the top with our own emotions, we can sometimes throw them at someone else. Psychologists call this 'projection' because it's as if we are projecting the movie of how we feel onto the other person. Making someone else feel bad too can give us a tiny moment of relief from our feelings, but then we end up feeling even worse.

Maybe you can think of times in your life when you've been unkind to someone because you got into a difficult, stressful situation. Perhaps you had a bad day at school and took it out on your mum by shouting at her. It's not how you usually behave, or how you want to behave, and you probably felt bad about it later, but at the time you weren't thinking about your behaviour, you were just reacting to your emotions. That's not an excuse. It was still the wrong thing to do and you should try to act better, but you wouldn't be human if you didn't get stuff wrong.

Parents can also make bad decisions about how they act when they are under stress. A family split is a horrible time for everyone involved and your parents may be arguing a lot and doing things you know they shouldn't.

PARENTS BEHAVING BADLY
Some things parents might do when they are splitting up:

* Say mean things about each other
* Tell lies about each other
* Argue and fight
* Gossip to their friends about the other parent
* Cry and shout

* Sulk and refuse to speak to each other
* Take things which belong to the other parent
* Spy on each other
* Read each other's text messages and emails
* Say mean things about the other parent's family and friends
* Slam doors, bang cupboards and clatter plates
* Swear
* Tell lies about where they've been
* Stay out late/all night

Wow! That's enough bad behaviour to put them on the naughty step for a year! These things don't always happen, of course – some couples manage to stay on polite and friendly terms and work things out in a very grown-up manner. But most parents do have at least a few big disagreements and if you have witnessed any of this sort of behaviour then you will know how upsetting it is. It can feel as if your parents have completely forgotten how adults should behave. At least you now know your parents are definitely human beings and, like human beings everywhere, they make mistakes. Even the best parents in the world can mess things up.

Remember: No one's perfect, we are all just humans doing our best.

WHAT'S THE STORY?

If you were an explorer looking over a cliff you might think, 'Wow! That's a long way down.' But if you were a monkey on a tree by the cliff looking across, you might think, 'Wow! That's a long way up.' And you would be right both times, because it depends where you're looking at things from. It comes down to your point of view.

There are also different ways of looking at things that happen in life, and so your parents will probably have different stories about what happened in their relationship.

Your father spent too much!

He was always complaining about something!

He's lazy!

His family never liked me!

Your mother was always going on about money!

She never listened!

She doesn't know how to relax!

She refused to get on with my family!

If your parents tell you different stories and you don't know who to believe it can feel very uncomfortable. But sometimes there's no one person who's right or one person who's wrong. It depends on your point of view. Both your parents might think they're right but they're only seeing it from one side. You don't have to decide who's telling the truth or whose 'side' you are

on. You can have your own point of view, the point of view of a child who loves both of them and doesn't want to be a part of the argument. If you find yourself being asked to take sides, simply say, 'That's grown-up stuff.'

Grab a Pen!

Think about what you know about your parents' relationship. Write their story or draw it in pictures or on a timeline if you prefer. Here are some prompts to help:

* Where did they meet?
* How old were they?
* When did they marry or move in together?
* When were you born?
* What did they like to do?
* When did they split up?
* Why do you think they split up?

If there is anything you don't know or understand you can ask your parents. There will probably be some parts of their story which are different from each other but that's OK. It's because they are seeing it from different points of view. You might be able to understand that better than they can.

Thinking Differently

At times it's hard to see things from another person's point of view. We sometimes call it putting yourself in someone else's shoes. If it helps, literally stand in your mum's or dad's shoes and pretend to be them. How do they see things?

Maybe you think your mum shouts a lot these days. Perhaps this is because she is tired or finding it difficult to manage all the stress at the moment. Perhaps the reason your dad hasn't been in touch for a couple of weeks is because he feels a bit of time out will help things calm down.

If we can understand other people's perspectives it makes it easier to then understand why they act in a certain way.

STAYING TRUE TO YOURSELF

If there is a lot of stress and arguing between your parents, you may feel like the only person acting like an adult is you. You may even wonder why you should carry on trying to behave well if they don't? The answer is that it's really important now, more than ever, to be your true self.

TRY THIS

Your Personal Guide

When adventurers attempt to climb Mount Everest, they usually take a guide, or Sherpa, with them. These local guides are highly skilled climbers and know the best routes to take to the top of that treacherous mountain. They make sure the climbers stay on the right path and don't get lost on the way to the summit.

When our parents split up it can feel like we are climbing a mountain without a guide. No one knows quite where they are supposed to be, where they're going, or the best route to get there. A useful way to help you find the right path again is to touch base with your values. Our values are like our personal guides. They are things that matter to us in the way we live our lives and how we treat others. Values help you to know which track to take at a crossroads and help you get through the twists and turns and steep climbs ahead.

Look at the list below and pick out three values you think are really important to you. There will probably be more than three, but don't worry too much, just pick a few that you think really matter to you.

Fairness   Kindness   Respect

Love   Honesty   Gratitude

Self-respect   Humour

Fun   Responsibility

Friendliness

Determination

Caring   Patience

Look at the values you have chosen. These are things that matter to you deeply. If you stay true to those values, you will feel much happier in yourself – even if the whole world seems to be acting strangely. For example, if you think it's important to tell the truth, be kind and respect other people, then carry on doing that, regardless of how people around you are behaving.

Your values are like a Sherpa guide pointing out the path you need to follow. Other people might not follow the same path but that's up to them – as long as you stick to your values they will guide you in the right direction. Sometimes you might lose your way, but thinking about your values will put you back on the right route.

If you live by your values, you will always end up feeling proud and happy with yourself.

PARENTS BEHAVING BADLY – PART 2!

Oh, yes. Sorry. There's more!

Even when your parents have separated and are living in different homes, there can still be misunderstandings – and often it's you that gets stuck in the middle.

Perhaps he's just making conversation, but if your dad asks, 'How's your mum's new job going?' you can't help but hear alarm bells ring. What's the right thing to say? Does Mum want me to discuss her job? Will she be annoyed that me and Dad are talking about her? Will it make Dad sad if I tell him how much happier she is now?

The whole situation can feel very uncomfortable. Whatever you do or don't say is going to cause a problem. You love both your parents and don't want to do the wrong thing or to upset either of them.

And that's not the only way they do it. What about when one of your parents asks you to give the other one a message?

'Tell your dad he needs to sign those papers I sent him.'

'Tell your mother I need my books from the attic.'

Or when one parent buys you something and the other parent doesn't like it?

'Those trainers are bad for your feet.'

'Your father shouldn't be buying you sweets.'

Or when one parent says mean things about the other?

'Your father is completely irresponsible!'

'Your mother is wasting money again!'

Urgh! Parents. STOP!

This is no way for adults to behave. They may not realise what they are doing but if you're in the middle of your parents' petty rows and attempts to find out information it can feel like you're being pulled back and forth in a tug-of-war by a bunch of rowdy pirates.

As we've said before, you can't control how other people are acting but you can control how you behave and respond. If your parents are putting you in the middle, you are allowed to tell them to stop. You are not a carrier pigeon!

Speak to your parents about the things that are upsetting you and how you feel when you're stuck in the middle or asked to take sides. If it feels like too big a deal to speak to them face to face, try a message or a letter. They will probably be surprised and say they didn't realise they were doing it. If a similar situation arises again, simply say:

'You need to speak to Mum/Dad about that.'

That's all you have to say. You're not being rude, you're just being clear. Practise saying this sentence out loud, so you get confident enough to say it when you need to.

It Happened to Me

Keisha's Story

Keisha felt really awkward when she visited her dad one evening.

It was fine, we had a nice tea and a good laugh playing Uno, then when he was driving me home he suddenly said, 'So, does your mum have a new boyfriend?' I didn't know what to say, I just sort of shrugged but then he said, 'Does that mean yes?'

My mum had been out with someone from work a few times but I didn't really know much about it, it might have just been her friend. I didn't want to tell Dad a lie, but then what if he got really sad or mad if I told him the truth? Luckily, we pulled up outside the house and I just got out quickly. I worried about it all week in case he started asking me when I went around again, but I couldn't say anything to Mum because she'd just get cross about it. It just felt like I was stuck in the middle and somehow it was all my problem now. In the end I put it in a text to Dad, saying I didn't want to talk about Mum any more. Next time I saw Dad he apologised and said he wasn't thinking straight, and it wouldn't happen again.

Psychologists have a long word for when parents put you in the middle. They call it **triangulation** – because instead of the information flowing smoothly between your parents, it has to go around sharp corners like a triangle. Unfortunately for you, it's not very comfortable being the third point in that triangle. Practising your communication skills and sticking to your values will help you to get out of it.

Hard as all this is, try to remember that your parents are not acting normally right now. It can be worrying to watch them act like this, but it won't last forever. Underneath it all your parents are still the same people they've always been, and they will get back to being that person again. They both love you very much.

Survival Kit Essentials

1. RECOGNISE THAT THERE ARE DIFFERENT POINTS OF VIEW.
   You don't have to decide who's right or choose a side.

2. EXPLAIN HOW YOU FEEL. Your parents are doing this because they have their own communication difficulties and they don't realise how it is making you feel. Use the communication skills you have learned to explain.

3. REMEMBER, it is not fair for your parents to expect you to be the go-between, so it's important that it stops.

4. FIND YOUR VALUES. Identify what really matters to you and stay true to yourself.

5. REFUSE TO GET INVOLVED. Practise saying, 'You'll have to speak to Mum/Dad about that.'

SAY IT OUT LOUD!

'I'm going to leave it up to the grown-ups to communicate between themselves. I'm not a carrier pigeon! I will let them know what my feelings are and I will try hard to see things from their point of view when I can.'

CHAPTER SEVEN

BORDER CROSSINGS
HOW TO NEGOTIATE
DIFFERENT HOUSE RULES

'There's NO place like home.
There's NO place like home.'

Dorothy, *The Wizard of Oz*

First the good news. When your parents live in different homes you get two sets of birthday presents! You might also get double festivities and presents for Christmas or the other holidays your family celebrates. Win-win! Having two homes definitely has its upside. Two places to hang out, two different bedrooms and different activities, toys and tech to enjoy. It also usually means you get to spend more time with each of your parents on their own.

All good so far.

But (you knew there'd be a but, right?) it's probably fair to say that if your parents agreed on everything, they wouldn't have split up in the first place. So, it's very likely, when it comes to your different homes, there will also be two different sets of rules, and in the same way as you have to obey different laws in different countries, you have to learn the particular rules of your parents' homes. That can take a bit of getting used to.

Thinking Differently

Did you know that these laws exist in different countries?

* In Singapore it's illegal to chew gum.
* In Dubai it's illegal to have a dirty car.
* In Germany it's illegal to use a drill on a Sunday.
* In Barbados it's illegal to wear camouflage-patterned clothing.

* In the UK it's illegal to 'handle a salmon in suspicious circumstances'!

See if you can work out what the reasons behind these odd-sounding rules might be. (Answers can be found on page 159.)

As you can see, these rules might not always seem sensible at first but most of them have a good reason behind them. In a similar way, your parents will probably have different rules in each of their homes. They will each have good reasons for putting those rules in place, but it can become very confusing to have to keep switching back and forth.

'Shoes off in the house, please!'

'It's 9.00pm. Lights off, you know the rule.'

'Homework before screen time.'

'Dirty clothes belong in the washing basket!'

'Can you go back and make your bed, please?'

'No eating in the car!'

'Put the lid on the toothpaste!'

If the rules aren't the same in both homes, it can be easy to forget what you are and aren't allowed to do, and then it can seem like someone is always having a go at you for something.

There are a couple of things you can do to help make things run a little more smoothly. First of all, be a little flexible and give it time. When parents first have their own spaces they may be keen to lay down the law, but they will probably relax a bit when they settle in.

If your parents have a good relationship, you can ask them to talk about it between the two of them and make some decisions. It's much easier if everyone agrees the same 'lights out' time, then you know where you stand and can't get in trouble. Unfortunately, as we've seen in previous chapters, separating parents are often not that good at communicating and, if that's the case, once again you are going to have to take a big breath and accept it for now.

Grab a Pen!

Working Out the Rules

In your journal, make a list of all the different rules in your parents' homes.

Have a look at the list and decide which ones you think you could probably keep at both homes without too much bother. For example, if one parent has a 'no phones at the table' rule, it would be easy enough to keep to that rule in your other parent's home too. This is something you could do to make things easier for everyone, including yourself, and it would be a good habit to get into anyway.

Compromise

Now write down the rules you could compromise on. For example, if one of your parents thinks you should get one hour's screen time a night but you don't think that's enough, what would you settle for? Could you manage with one hour if you could get longer at weekends?

Now look if there are any rules you think are really unfair. Maybe you have to go to bed at the same time as your little sister at your mum's home and you think this is really not right. Write down the rules you think really need to totally change and why you think they are unfair.

Negotiate

Now is the time to dust off your negotiation skills! When you have got all your reasons sorted out, use your Three-Step Communication Plan (see pages 59–61) to talk about the rules. Or write it all out in a letter and give it to the parent concerned. Explain where you have tried to keep to the same rules in both houses and where you are trying hard to make a compromise. Then give your reasons why you think some things are really unfair.

Parents may not even have realised they were giving you mixed messages. You probably won't get all the changes you want but you might get some, and at the very least you will get to understand your parents' reasons for having those the rules. At the end of the day, it's a parent's job to set rules and boundaries and there are some you are just going to have to put up with. The better you get at communication, though, the more your point of view will be heard.

Remember: Unlike you, your parents are not spending time in one another's homes, so they have no idea what the rules are in each place. Let your parents know what it feels like for you, and how things could be changed for the better.

MY FAVOURITE HOME

Another issue you may have when you first have two homes is finding you prefer one place to another. Usually, if one of your parents has stayed in the family home, it just feels more familiar when you're there, so it's more comfortable to hang out in. As well as this, one of your parents may have more money than the other to buy nice things and keep their place warm, or more time to make it look nice and keep it clean. One of your parents may just be better than the other at 'homemaking', or be much more into technology and have a great TV and gaming set-up. One parent might have to work when you're there while the other has more time to chill out with you. One place may have a lot more of your things in it, too. It's only natural to prefer being at one place to another for a while. But a home isn't just about stuff, it's about people, and both your homes have people who love you and want to spend time with you. Give it time and put up with a few inconveniences for a while – it's always a bit strange getting used to a new home.

In the meantime, be clear with your parents about what personal possessions you want in each home and about not throwing things out if they are important to you. If you want to you could keep a special box of your important things in each place. Slide it under the bed or keep it on a shelf and make sure everyone knows it is your important stuff which no one is allowed to touch. You could also offer to help decorate your room, to make it feel more familiar. It won't be long before you're feeling right at home!

It Happened to Me

Gabriel's Story

Gabriel was getting to the stage where he was dreading going to his dad's flat.

When my parents first split up, I didn't like going to my dad's new flat. It was kind of depressing. He didn't have much furniture and it was like he couldn't be bothered to decorate or keep it nice. I didn't think he'd ever be the sort of person to live like that, it made me feel sorry for him too. At home our house felt pretty much the same, but going to my dad's just made me feel sad and gloomy. One weekend it was raining loads when I went to stay and we couldn't go anywhere. I suggested we could paint the living room. I said I'd seen this really nice yellow colour on an advert. Dad said no at first but then he said, 'Why not?' We went to the DIY shop and got paint and brushes and it was really fun, by the end of the weekend we had done the whole room. When I went back next time Dad said he had a surprise. He had bought new curtains and two new chairs, and he had put lots of pictures up – the room looked great. Now we are planning on tackling my bedroom!

KEEPING TRACK OF YOUR STUFF

Another common problem around having two homes is keeping track of your stuff. It's so easy to forget to take your school shoes to your dad's or leave your maths book at your mum's and end up in trouble at home and school. This is when it's important to get mega-organised.

Grab a Pen!

When you pack your bag for an expedition you need a list of everything you need so you don't forget anything vital. Going from one parent's home to another may not be quite the same as climbing Kilimanjaro, but getting organised can definitely save you a mountain of stress!

YOUR SUPER-ORGANISER PLAN!

Step One

Make a list of all the simple things you need at both houses. Below are some suggestions:

* Toothbrush
* Hairbrush
* Pyjamas
* Toiletries
* Paper, pens and other stationery
* Wellies
* Games
* Spare clothes

Now make a list of stuff you need to take back and forth. Here are some suggestions:

* Mobile
* Earphones
* Cuddly monkey
* School shoes
* School uniform
* Homework
* PE kit
* Coat

Show your list to your parents and ask them to help you get it sorted out. For more expensive things, for example, a bike or a laptop, you might have to come to a sharing arrangement, or wait until your birthday, but having the basics will get rid of a lot of small irritations.

Step Two

For the next step it's time to get into organised mode again.

Make sure you've got a calendar with when you'll be at each house clearly marked out. This can be a calendar on the wall, a piece of paper on the fridge or a calendar in your mobile. Mark out when you are at each house clearly, with a different-colour pen or different filler.

Step Three

The day/night before you are going to the other house, use the calendar and the lists to check what you need to pack. Tick things off as you pack them.

Step Four (this is the
secret but most important part of this process). Give yourself a massive pat on the back for being an Organising Superstar!

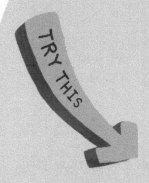

Look at this list of eight items for just a few seconds.

Now cover it and see how many things you can remember.

- ✳ Banana
- ✳ Sunglasses
- ✳ Guitar
- ✳ Sunshine
- ✳ Pebble
- ✳ Shoe
- ✳ Torch
- ✳ Present

When you have a list of things you need to remember it can be helpful to imagine them all together. For example, for this list you could imagine a banana, wearing sunglasses, playing the guitar, in the sunshine, with a pebble in its shoe, who's just been given a torch as a present!

Try it.

Did you remember more? What's the longest list you can remember?

Survival Kit Essentials

1. BE FLEXIBLE. Try not to get too hung up on the rules and arrangements for now. Everyone's in the process of creating a new normal.

2. NEGOTIATE. Use your communication skills to talk to your parents, but remember it's their job to set rules and boundaries.

3. GET SUPER-ORGANISED. Ask parents to make sure essential items are available at both homes and make a changeover-day tick-list.

SAY IT OUT LOUD!

'This is such a new situation for all of us. It will take time to get used to it. I'm going to use my super new organisation and communication skills to make things easier for me and to let people know what I need.'

CHAPTER EIGHT

NEW CREW MEMBERS
HOW TO MANAGE RELATIONSHIPS WITH NEW PARTNERS AND THEIR CHILDREN

'There's not a word yet for OLD FRIENDS who've just met.'

Gonzo, *The Muppet Movie*

It's almost certain to happen at some point, maybe sooner or maybe later ... one or both of your parents will start a relationship with a new partner. Here we go again, another change in the weather! And maybe these new partners will also have children of their own. Suddenly there's a whole new family set-up and it can be hard to be sure where you're meant to fit in or even if there's still space for you at all. It's perfectly understandable if you feel a bit confused or resentful, but before you make any snap judgements about these new crew members, drop your anchor, take a breath of sea air (or whatever air you have handy) and have a think about the situation.

First of all, there's lots of good news. Your parent still loves you. That won't change, no matter how many new people turn up in their lives. Love isn't like an almost empty jar of Nutella, that you have to spread thinner and thinner just to make it go around. Love is like a magic jar, that just makes more and more to share. Your parent has always loved you and always will.

And you love them too, right?

Grab a Pen!

Write down a quick list of reasons why you love your parent. All their good qualities. Here are some ideas but you can add your own:

I love my mum/dad because they are …

Kind   Caring   Good at making things

Funny   A great cook

Energetic   Creative   Patient

Thoughtful   Fun to play with

A good Listener   Good playing at sport with me

Wow! That's one great parent. And whatever qualities you love in your parent will be what their new partners love too. So, you've already got something in common with the new person – you both think your mum or dad is great!

The new person in your parent's life has probably made them happier too, which is great for them, right? Everyone deserves a chance to find the right partner and feel loved. And happier parents are much more fun to be around.

So far, so good. But even though your parent may be happy, things can be a bit more complicated for you. Sometimes a new partner arrives on the scene and just fits right in. You might find you like them and get on with them from the first meeting. That's great – you can probably skip this chapter! But if you find you are struggling with your feelings about them, you are not alone. Most people find that it takes time to get used to having a new person around.

One difficult situation that often happens is when the new partner is seen as the reason why your parents separated in the first place. Maybe things seemed fine until they came along and 'split your parents up'. You are bound to feel angry with them and your other parent may well be extremely hurt or angry too. What a complicated mass of feelings!

To help calm things down, take another breath of sea air and think about

the facts. Even if this new person was the final reason one of your parents left home, people usually only find new boyfriends or girlfriends because they are unhappy in their present relationship and are looking for something different. Thinking back, you may be able to see that your parents were already having problems, or maybe they were doing an excellent job of hiding them from you. Either way, it can't all be the fault of one person.

Your parents would almost certainly have split up anyway and this new person just moved things on. Both your parents are great people, but they just weren't meant to be together. It's fine to feel sad about this but not helpful to keep hold of angry feelings and blame.

At first, having a new 'parent' figure can bring up all sorts of feelings. You may feel you don't need another parent in your life, or that they are 'taking over' your parent, taking up too much of their time and interfering in your family. You might find it difficult to understand why your parent likes them so much and cringe when your parent giggles, cuddles or makes those funny eyes at their new partner. You might not even like them *at all!*

All these feelings are understandable. It can be tough to allow a new person into your family. Our natural, tribal instinct is to look at them as some sort of outsider, trying to intrude into our space. It can hurt to accept that your parent is moving on to a new phase in their life, or make you cross that things are changing yet again. Sometimes young people think that if they sulk, strop and be mean about this person for long enough, their parent will realise how truly awful they are and dump them. But that rarely happens.

Parents make decisions based on how they feel, and they will put your reaction down to you just not knowing their new partner well enough yet, or even that you're just being 'difficult', while you may be feeling as though you've been pushed aside and your parent now gets to be happy while you feel miserable.

It's as if you're looking at things through different lenses. Your parent is wearing rose-coloured, heart-shaped glasses, seeing only the good things ahead, but you may feel like you're wearing goggles fogged up with worries and sadness. None of these emotions are easy to manage, and if you feel angry or sad, remember to revisit the exercises in previous chapters to help you.

Often, when our parents are single, we get used to being treated more like a friend or a mini grown-up when we spend time with them. Maybe watching TV with them, cooking tea or making decisions about where to go on holiday. If this has happened, it can feel even harder when a real-life grown-up comes along and they start doing things with them. This can feel like yet another rejection. But, if you look at it in another way, although you might enjoy this close time with your parent, you won't want to still be curled up with your dad watching *Antiques Roadshow* when you're seventeen. Your parents need to find friends their own age. You are not being replaced – you are being freed up to carry on with your own life.

Remember: Moving on does not mean moving away. Your mum is still able to be your mum even if she is in love with a new partner (as well as George Clooney and your maths teacher and that guy off *Bake Off*).

As life gets busier with all of these new people, you and your parent may have to work extra hard to still find time to be together, just you and them. Explain to your parent that this is still important to you, even if you do enjoy time all together as a family. This special time, just you and them, might be 30 minutes every Tuesday when you wait for your sports class to start, or baking together every other Saturday afternoon. Make this part of your routine of being in that house. It will recharge your batteries and remind you of how special you still are.

At times like this, more than ever, your parents may need reminding of how you're feeling. Let them know if you feel awkward seeing them kissing and hugging their new partner, or sad when Dad's new girlfriend picks you up from your Saturday match instead of him. Parents can be so delighted with their new relationship that they forget to consider that it might not feel the same from your point of view.

In the end, even if they really annoy you, if this new person is going to be around for a while, you only have two choices:

1. You can either fight to the bitter end and make yourself, and everyone around you, sad and cross,

OR...

2. You can accept that this is yet another change and make an effort to come to terms with it.

Let's be honest, dealing with change is one of the things you're pretty good at now. You can use your new skills to be flexible, open up a bit and give this person a chance. This doesn't mean you have to jump into their arms every time you see them (your mum or dad probably do enough of that kind of embarrassing stuff themselves) but it does mean saying hello to them, answering their questions and showing some interest in being with them.

Do you remember when we talked about different perspectives? This is another situation where you will need to work hard to see things from someone else's point of view. Perhaps some of the annoying things this new person does is just their way of trying to fit in. Try thinking about how the world looks from where they're standing.

Thinking Differently

Some of the reasons people behave the way they do.

If they are . . .	We might think	But maybe it's because they . . .
Really quiet, don't speak to you much, only speak to your parent	They don't like me and can't be bothered with me	Don't want to overwhelm you, feel awkward, are not sure what to say, feel shy, haven't spent much time with young people, are not sure if you want to chat with them
Overfriendly, always talking to you, asking you lots of questions	They're pushy and they're trying to make me like them	Are trying hard to be friends, want to show you they like you, interested in finding out about you
Bossy, telling you what to do, acting like your parent	They don't' have the right to tell me what to do – I already have parents!	Want to fit in as part of the family, aren't very confident about how to act, want to show they know how to be a parent (even if they really don't!)

| Always hugging and cuddling with your parent, embarrassingly lovey-dovey! | They're just rubbing in the fact that they're happy and I'm not | Are in love! |

The more we think about why someone might be acting in a certain way, the more we can understand and get to know them better. Imagine how it must be from their side. You are the person your parent loves the most in the world, so they will be desperate to make the right impression, but if you've ever been in a situation where you were trying to make a good impression such as meeting someone important, or famous even, you'll know that we often end up trying so hard we don't act like ourselves.

Give them some time and a chance to get to know you, and you might find they become much more relaxed and fun to be around. You may never end up wearing the rosy glasses your parent does, but over time yours will defog and you will be able to see the new partner for who they are, and for how they make your parent feel.

Getting to Know You
One way to get people to relax and chat is to get them talking about themselves. They are on safe territory there and know what they are talking about. To do this, the best way is to ask questions.

Any sort of questions are fine but the best sort to get people chatting are called open-ended questions. These are questions where you can't just answer 'yes' or 'no' but have to give a little explanation. To ask an open-ended question just start with What, When, Who, Why or How. Try it! Think of three questions you could ask the new person next time you meet.

Here are some examples:

* Who is your favourite singer or band?
* What sort of food do you like best?
* Why did you decide to become a nurse?

SPECIAL NOTE

Step-parents often get a bad rap. But many turn out to be a great extra adult in your life. If your parent hasn't listened to your point of view on something, or is arguing with your other parent, a step-parent can often be the one who smooths things over and takes a more balanced point of view.

However, as Cinderella found out, not all step-parents and new partners are great. Occasionally the new person can turn out to be unkind to you or downright nasty. If this happens, you must tell someone – tell your other parent, a teacher at school or a friend. They will help you figure out the best plan of action. You don't have to put up with mean or violent behaviour, even if other people in your family are.

STEP-SIBLINGS

Along with new adults, we can also end up with new step-siblings. This can be great fun, especially if they are around your age – you might end up with a new best friend. However, just like any brother or sister, you might not get on so well. They might have completely different interests, or having them in the family means you have to share a room. Once they are part of your family, though, there's not much you can do about it so, once again, you have those two choices – get your acceptance hat on and make the most of having someone to play computer games or watch *Strictly* with, or start an attack of the sulks, which will only make you more unhappy in the long run.

Use the same technique of asking questions and letting them talk about themselves. Try to find things you have in common, such as music or games you like – then you'll always have something to chat about. One way of starting a conversation is to mention something of theirs that you like, for example, 'I really like your trainers/bag/jacket. Where did you get it?'

Time is also a great way of forging new bonds – just hanging out together, or going into town together, sitting watching TV together. You don't have to be talking, but just sharing experiences can help build up a connection.

Don't forget, they will also have been through a family split and may have feelings and experiences similar to yours. They probably never asked for a whole new set of siblings. They may feel caught in the middle or hurt and rejected. They may also find it hard to trust anyone any more.

Just like with a step-parent, these step-siblings can add to your life rather than take away from it. You just need to dig deep into that pot of acceptance you have found and use your energy not to fight this, but to cope with it. Make an effort and, when you get to know them better, you might find they are more interesting than you thought.

It Happened to Me

Asha's Story

Asha had always wanted a brother or sister but three years ago, when she was eight, her parents split up.

My dad left my mum because he had a new girlfriend. It was awful. My mum was so sad, she kept crying. Then she got really mad and wouldn't talk to him, or even answer the door when he picked me up. When I went to his house it was so awkward because his new girlfriend was there and I didn't know what to say to her and I hated her for taking my dad away. Then things got even worse! My mum also met someone else and he had a teenage daughter, Kya. It was like all these new people were in my family and I didn't even know where I belonged. I didn't really like mum's boyfriend either to start off with, he was kind of serious and nothing like my dad, and I was worried about meeting Kya. I thought she might be really bossy, or think I was a little brat! When I did meet her, I just tried to smile, and I said I liked her jeans. But I didn't need to worry, she was fun.

She did my hair in braids and helped me with a model space rocket I was trying to make. After that she always came with her dad and when I saw how well she got on with him I started to realise he was actually pretty nice too, just quiet. Now my mum has got married again so Kya is my proper step-sister, which is very cool. I began to realise that my mum and dad were both great people but they just weren't suited to each other. It wasn't really anyone's fault. It took a bit of getting used to but I get on fine with my dad's girlfriend now. And she and my dad have just had a baby boy, so now I'm a big sister too! I never thought I'd have any siblings and now I've got two.

SHARING SPACES

If you have to share a bedroom with a step-sibling, the two of you will have to make some rules about sharing. If you are able to agree this on your own, that's great, but if not ask your parent to help you. Think about the things you are happy to share and what things are yours alone. For example, you might be happy to share books and games but not your art supplies. Make sure you both have a space to store things that are private to you and that the other person knows not to touch. You could also talk about keeping the space tidy and what rules you want to agree on that. Respect the other person's things and they should respect yours. If they don't, speak to your parent about it. Remember that you are fellow travellers in this whole

situation. You have both been through the same thing – your parents have split up and met new partners. You may be very different in some ways, but you probably have more insight into how the other is feeling than anyone else does.

Having a new, blended family can be a challenge at first, but it can bring a lot of positives in the long run. More people to have fun with, more people to talk things through with, happier parents and a more stable and relaxed home. Speak to friends who have been in your situation. How did they manage the ups and downs? How do they feel about things now? Giving it time, understanding your emotions and thinking about things from other people's point of view can help you get through these new turbulent waters to calmer times beyond.

Survival Kit Essentials

1. LOOK FOR THE POSITIVES IN THE SITUATION. When your parents are happy, they are more likely to be relaxed and cheerful.

2. TALK OUT YOUR FEELINGS WITH YOUR PARENT. They may not have considered how you feel.

3. TRY TO LOOK AT THE SITUATION from other people's point of view, even if you don't agree with it.

4. MAKE AN EFFORT to get to know the new people in your family. Once they relax you might find you like them better.

5. KEEP YOUR PERSONAL SPACE. Make some rules and boundaries to keep your private possessions your own.

6. TALK TO OTHERS WHO HAVE BEEN IN THIS SITUATION. They will help you to see that things can get better, that new family members can bring lots of good things too.

SAY IT OUT LOUD!

'I know it takes time to get to know people, but I think it will be worth the effort in the end.'

CHAPTER NINE

TIME TRAVELLING
HOW TO DEAL WITH WORRIES ABOUT FUTURE RELATIONSHIPS

'We have an opportunity to create the FUTURE and decide what that's like.'

Dr Mae C. Jemison, astronaut and scientist

It can be fun to think about the future.

What job will I do? Where will I live? Will I travel the world? Will I get married? Will I have children? Will I be rich? Will I go into space? Will I be a world champion uni-cyclist?

Hey. Anything's possible, right?!

Thinking Differently

These famous people had very different lives when they were young. Did they ever imagine their amazing futures?

* Daniel Craig is rich and famous for playing James Bond in the films but early in his acting career he earned so little money it's said he sometimes had to sleep on a park bench.

* Writer J.K. Rowling was a single mum, struggling to make ends meet and living in a tiny flat, while she wrote the first Harry Potter book.

* As a child, superstar singer Justin Bieber was frequently hungry. He didn't even have a bedroom, he had to sleep on a pull-out couch.

* Outstanding Olympian Sir Mo Farah spent his early childhood as a refugee in Djibouti before moving to London, where he couldn't speak a word of English. As a teenager he worked in McDonalds to earn his keep.

Young people who have been involved in a family separation occasionally have thoughts about the future too – less positive ones. Especially when thinking about future relationships. It can seem sometimes, when you're in the middle of a messy family split-up, that all relationships are doomed to fail, you can't trust anyone, so it would be easier if everyone stayed single forever. If this thought has been circling around in your head, then it's time to kick it out.

First of all, you are not your parents. Sure, you have a bit of each of their DNA in your make-up, but you also have a lot of other things which make you, you. All sorts of things influence how we feel and think about the world. Friends, teachers, grandparents, social media, books, film, TV, video games, sports, art, music and the John Lewis Christmas advert – the list of things that go to make up who we are is endless. This all goes to make you into a completely unique person – with your own thoughts and ideas and the free will to make your own decisions. **Fantastic!**

Your parents are also unique individuals. They tried to make their relationship work but in the end it didn't. Sometimes we find the right person for us and sometimes we don't. Sometimes that person is the right companion for us on a certain part of our life journey, but then our paths take different directions. That doesn't mean the whole relationship was a mistake. Your parents had you, and that was a great thing that happened to them – and pretty good for you too! So even though things didn't work out perfectly, it was a good job they took the chance.

No matter how difficult your parents' relationship, you are not destined to repeat it. No one can foresee the future, but you can be certain that your story will be completely your own. Which is kind of exciting!

131

Remember: Your future isn't mapped out.
It's yours to create!

Another thing to consider is that by now you have a lot of experience about what makes a relationship work. You may not realise it, but your experiences have given you a much more mature understanding of life than many people your age – such as an acceptance that things aren't always going to go your way, skills in negotiating, compromising and communicating, and a sense of gratitude for things that go well. All these skills mean that you are likely to build much stronger relationships and friendships in the future.

Grab a Pen!

Just like an adventurer who has had to deal with bad weather, difficult terrain and challenging conditions as they make their journey, you have also had to go through all sorts of tough experiences. You will have learned from every one of them and now have new skills to help you as you grow up. Think about some of the things you have learned. Write a list of the new knowledge and skills you have acquired on your journey so far. Here are some ideas:

- ✳ I know how to start a conversation with a new person.
- ✳ I know how to listen when someone is speaking about their feelings.
- ✳ I know when someone is feeling sad and what might cheer them up.

* I know how to negotiate rules.
* I am able to take responsibility for myself and my stuff.

Read through your list and feel proud of yourself – by now you are pretty much a friendship and family relationship expert!

It Happened to Me

Esther's Story

Esther didn't realise how much she had learned from her parents' divorce until her friend, Ellie, was going through the same thing.

Ellie didn't know how to speak to her mum and dad. She wanted to spend more time with her dad, but her parents had just arranged for her to go every other weekend. Her dad's early starts at work meant she couldn't stay over in the week because he couldn't drop her at school. If she went every weekend her mum would be upset. She felt like no one was listening to what she wanted.

I talked to her about what had worked for me – asking for a time to talk properly and writing down what I wanted to say so I didn't forget. Telling them your reasons and what you want to happen.

Ellie talked to her mum first. She wasn't upset, she was surprised. She hadn't realised it was bothering Ellie. She said that if her dad could find a way, she would be happy for her to go more often. Ellie's dad said he had just been trying to make things easy for everyone and didn't want to upset her routine, but if she wanted to stay over in the week, he'd try to arrange something with work.

Now Ellie sees her dad on Wednesdays too. She says I should be a professional problem-solver! I never realised how much I'd learned and I was super-happy that I could help.

THE SECOND WAVE

As time passes, you will find that you stop thinking about your parents' separation so much.

You will start getting used to your new family arrangements. You will start to think of your second home as home too and not be so worried about only seeing your pet tortoise every other week. Things will seem to be moving on at last and you may think you've come to the end of the journey. However, sometimes an unexpected event can trigger those feelings to come back again. This doesn't always happen but it's as well to be prepared if it does.

For example: Your friend is mean and says they don't want to hang out with you any more.

Whoosh!

Like a tidal wave washing over you, everything comes back. You're not only feeling hurt by your friend, but on top of that you remember all the other feelings of sadness and rejection you felt when your mum and dad split up. It's as if your brain had all these feelings stored up and it's swept you right back to the start of your journey.

If this happens to you, stay calm, take big slow breaths and remember all of the things you have already learned. One of the most important things to remember is that this wave of emotion will pass, just like all the other waves have. Feelings come and go, like a tide that ebbs and flows. It's not going to drown you – you are very strong after all your experiences. It will hurt for a while and then the feelings will ease. Remember to be extra, extra kind to yourself. Find your list of nice things and treat yourself to a bigger spoonful of marshmallows in your hot chocolate, watch that film you used to love when you were four and hug your dog (or tortoise) even more than usual.

KNOW YOUR BRILLIANCE

Your parent's job is to look after you, right? But, as we've seen, your parent is only human and only has one brain. When their heads are full of thoughts about where to live, how to earn money and feelings such as anger and sadness, your parents may have less space to think about you and what you need. At times like this, it can be easy for us to think that if we were somehow better children, nicer, more helpful, more loveable, then our parents would have more time for us, pay us more attention. But the truth is, you could be the most perfect kid in the world, and your parent would still only have one, very full-up brain. Remember, none of this is happening because of you, it's happening because your parents fell out of love and they now have a lot to sort out. They will get back to their old selves soon but in the meantime, why not remind yourself of what is good about you?

We're not so good at thinking about our strengths. We can list off everyone else's – Lori is brilliant at netball, Reuben knows loads about music, Gavrill is great at maths – but we're not so used to stopping and thinking of what is good about us.

Now is the time to make your own advert, advertising YOU! Write down all the things you are good at, all the things that are important to you and all the things that you enjoy. Being good doesn't necessarily mean being in the top team or getting 99 per cent. Being good at something means you really give it a go.

No one can do more than their best, so even if you only get 30 per cent, if that's your best shot, then you've done great.

Being good at stuff is not just school or sports – how about remembering that you are a great friend, an excellent listener, a superb brother or sister or the greatest cheese-and-tomato toastie maker!

Once you've written your list, draw a picture of your advert, or a series of pictures. Give it a headline and remember to list your great points. Here are some words you could use:

Great   Amazing   Stupendous

Super   Stunning   Awesome

Remarkable   Fabulous   The best

Breath-taking   Fantastic

You could even film it and make it a TV advert!

When you feel sad and lonely, and your brain is chugging off down the track of 'No one likes me' or 'I'm rubbish at this' or 'Everything is my fault', pull out your advert and remind yourself how awesome you are and that you can learn to make yourself feel better as well as let others look after you.

Survival Kit Essentials

1. YOU ARE NOT YOUR MUM/DAD. You are a unique person and can make your own way in the world however you decide.

2. RECOGNISE YOUR SKILLS. You have a great set of skills which makes you a 'relationship expert'!

3. WATCH OUT FOR EVENTS WHICH TRIGGER A SECOND WAVE OF SAD FEELINGS. Remember, it will pass.

4. REMIND YOURSELF THAT NONE OF THIS IS YOUR FAULT and that you are a super human being with lots of qualities, skills and experiences that make you someone special.

SAY IT OUT LOUD!

'I am wonderful, unique me! I am looking forward to using all of my new skills and experience in the future.'

CHAPTER TEN

WRITE YOUR OWN MAP
HOW TO MAKE YOUR OWN
SELF-SUPPORT PLAN

'We do not need magic to transform our world. We carry all the POWER we need inside ourselves already.'

J.K. Rowling

It's time to look at the bigger picture. Your parents' separation has been a rough ride, but it's only one part of the exciting, but sometimes bumpy, journey of your life. There will be challenges all through your life, but the skills you've learned can help you in lots of different ways. With the tools from your Survival Kit you can manage the high peaks and the low valleys, the choppy seas and the sudden storms, and even find your path again if you get lost in one of life's jungles!

The best way of making sure you have the right tools available to you is to make a plan. Your own Personal Action Plan!

Grab a Pen!
(In fact, grab all your pens – this is going to be fun!)

MAKING AN ACTION PLAN

Step One
First of all, we need to do a bit of thinking.

What are the things that are causing you a problem that you want to change? Write a list. Now choose a few that you'd like to tackle first – two or three is plenty. You can come back to look at the other things later. Be clear about what the actual issue is. Ask yourself 'Why?' questions to help yourself to dig down to what the real problem is. For example, if you wrote:

✳ 'I don't want to go to Dad's on Saturday.'
   <u>Think:</u> Why not?
✳ 'Because Dad's new partner will be there.'
   <u>Think:</u> Why does that matter?
✳ 'Because I don't think he likes me.'
   <u>Think:</u> Why do I think that?
✳ 'Because he's kind of quiet and doesn't say much.'

So, the real issue here is not that you want to avoid going to Dad's but that you need to build a better relationship with his new partner.

Make sure you dig down and think about what the real problem is in each situation. When you have got to the core of the problem, go on to the next stage.

Step Two

Find a clean double-page spread page in your journal and write 'My Action Plan!' at the top.

Then split the pages into four columns – two on each page –and add the following headings:

✳   Problems
✳   Actions
✳   Date
✳   Tick!

Use plenty of different colours and doodles – colourful things stick in our mind better!

For each problem think of two or three actions you could take to help make it better. The Survival Kit ideas at the end of each chapter can help you but you can use any ideas of your own too. There is no right and wrong here, it's just working the problem through. Be creative!

For example, if you think you need to get to know Dad's partner better, some possible actions could be:

✳ Smile and be friendly
✳ Try to think of things from his point of view, maybe he just feels awkward
✳ Ask him something about himself – use open-ended questions

Step Three
Put your actions into practice!

✳ Be brave and make a start
✳ Try to use these three Golden Rules: Communicate, Negotiate, Compromise

Step Four
Think about how your problem-solving ideas went.

What worked? What didn't work? What could you do differently next time?

For example: 'I tried to talk to Dad's new boyfriend.'

✳ What worked?

I was brave and asked him which football team he supports.
He was friendly and we had a bit of a chat.

✳ What didn't work?

He doesn't really like football, so we ran out of stuff to say
pretty quickly!

✳ What could you do differently next time?

We could talk about dogs, because he has one too.
Me and Dad could take him to a football match!

You can then add your new ideas to your Action Plan!

Step Five

Finally, remember to put a big, bright tick next to the actions you've done,
and reward yourself with something from your list of nice things for doing a
great job.

All the skills you have learned are what we call 'transferable'. This means
you can use the same method to tackle a different issue, not necessarily
to do with your parents' separation. For example, if you've used your
communication skills to talk to your parents about your feelings, well done!
Could you use a similar approach to talk to a friend or a teacher about a
problem you're having at school?

Maybe you've used your skills at starting a conversation to speak with your mum's new partner. You could use the same way to get to know the new girl at school.

The grounding and breathing exercises you've practised could also be super-helpful before taking a test or performing on stage.

This is another example of how far you've come and how much you've learned and matured in coping with your parents' separation – you can deal with anything now!

SAY IT OUT LOUD!

'I have my kit. I'm ready to go!'

CONCLUSION

NEW HORIZONS
POSITIVE THOUGHTS FOR THE FUTURE

'You're off to Great Places! Today is your day! Your mountain is waiting, So ... GET ON YOUR WAY!'

Dr Seuss, *Oh, The Places You'll Go!*

From the moment you found out your parents were separating you started on a journey. You've had to struggle through emotional storms and turbulent times. You've had to compromise, negotiate and be flexible. You may have had to meet and fit in with new family members, and you've had to find new ways to communicate with those you already knew. You've had bad days and found the strength to get through them, and supported other people when they weren't feeling so great. You've been sad but you've learned to look for the positives and be grateful.

Whatever place you are at now, whether you're still at the start of your journey or you've travelled a long way down the line, you will already have experienced a lot of ups and downs. There's still a long way to go – being the child of separated parents is something that brings new challenges all through your life, but it also brings some unexpected benefits.

In the same way that climbing mountains builds up muscles in your arms and legs, coming through any traumatic life event builds up your emotional muscles and makes you a stronger, more flexible and resilient person. You've found your way through some tough times and that means that in future you'll be able to deal with challenges in a more confident way, knowing you've got that inner strength. You will also be more empathic, which means you can see the point of view of other people and understand their feelings. And because of this you'll probably find that people trust you and come

to you for support when they have tough times – they know you won't let them down.

You will also probably find your relationship with each of your parents is closer. While your friends' married parents might still be treating them like little kids, you and your parents have had to learn to talk about some big life events and grown-up stuff. Because you've worked your way through this, your parents will respect you for it and be more open to discussing things and interested in your opinions in other areas.

Another big benefit can be having happier parents. Without the arguments and stress, you might begin to see a side to your parents you hadn't seen before, or at least for a long time, and you can relax and enjoy each other's company. Whereas previously your parents may have done things together, you now get more individual time to spend with them. This means you can enjoy double the activities, holidays and fun experiences!

If you're at the beginning of the separation voyage, you might still feel like you're in the middle of the storm, and it will be hard to see any benefits for now, but trust that things will settle down. Remember you are not alone. All along the path there are people ready to support you and point you in the right direction. Let your family, friends and teachers help you. As you get older you will look back on this time as a difficult journey but one that your family had to take. You will know how much you learned and grew as a person and you will always be proud of the way you came through.

GLOSSARY & RESOURCES

GLOSSARY

Words and phrases you might hear

CAFCASS This stands for the Children and Family Court Advisory and Support Service.

CHILD ARRANGEMENTS ORDER This is the plan which details where a child lives, who they have contact with and for how long (these used to be called contact orders).

CHILD MAINTENANCE Money that the parent who doesn't live with their child pays to the other to help look after them.

CONTACT A word used for times when parents see their children (this used to be called access).

CUSTODY A word sometimes used to mean which parent you live with.

DIVORCE This is when two people who have been married split up and become unmarried.

FAMILY COURT A special court which deals with family matters. Definitely not for putting people in prison!

MEDIATION When parents speak to a trained person called a mediator, to help them make a decision on something they are having trouble agreeing about.

PARENTAL RESPONSIBILITY The legal responsibility parents have to their children. Usually this is shared between both parents, even if they are divorced and not living together.

People you might meet or hear about

All these people are specially trained to work with parents and children and might support you and your family in different ways.

ARBITRATOR Since 2012 families can use an arbitrator rather than a judge to rule on what should happen.

BARRISTER Someone who works alongside the solicitor and speaks for people in court.

CAFCASS ADVISOR This is someone who will speak to you if the court asks them to find out some more about your situation.

JUDGE The senior person in a court who makes final decisions.

MAGISTRATE Some courts have three magistrates who make a decision instead of a judge.

MEDIATOR A person who helps parents come to decisions.

SOCIAL WORKER A person who works with children and families to make sure children are properly looked after.

SOLICITOR A person who deals with the legal side of separation. Both of your parents will probably have their own solicitor to help them sort things like money and housing. If they go to court a solicitor might speak for them or they might appoint a barrister.

RESOURCES

Useful organisations

CAFCASS This website has some sections for children involved in divorce and separation. www.cafcass.gov.uk

CHILDLINE A special organisation and helpline for children. www.childline.org Helpline: 0800 1111

DIVORCE AID Information for children, teens and parents about how to cope with divorce and separation. http://www.divorceaid.co.uk/child/child-notyourfault.htm

KIDSCAPE Information and advice for children on how to deal with bullying. https://www.kidscape.org.uk/advice/advice-for-young-people/

NYAS National Youth Advocacy Service Information and advice mainly aimed at children in care but also providing advice for children with questions about their parents' divorce. https://youngpeople.nyas.net Helpline: 0808 808 1001

Books you might like to read

Balding, Clare *Fall Off, Get Back on Again, Keep Going*

Huebner, Dawn *Outsmarting Worry: An Older Kid's Guide to Managing Anxiety*

Saad, Nadim, Annabel Rosenhead *Happy Confident Me Journal*

Syed, Matthew *You are Awesome: Find Your Confidence and Dare to be Brilliant at (Almost) Anything*

Quotes

INTRODUCTION: 'As soon as he saw the Big Boots, Pooh knew that an Adventure was going to happen.' *Winnie the Pooh* by A.A. Milne (Methuen: 1926)

CHAPTER 1: 'No matter how tall the mountain is, it cannot block the sun.' *Best Loved Chinese Proverbs* by Theodora Lau (HarperCollins: 1995)

CHAPTER 2: 'I'm not afraid of storms for I'm learning how to sail my ship.' *Little Women* by Louisa May Alcott (Robert Bros: 1868)

CHAPTER 3: 'You can't change conditions. Just the way you deal with them.' Jessica Watson OAM, Sailor. https://www.invictusgames2018.com/invictus-games-sydney-2018-crews-announced/

'The world is complicated, Bar. That's why it's interesting.' Barack Obama, Instagram 20.11.20. https://www.instagram.com/p/CHgbgIsjFjY/?utm_source=ig_embed

CHAPTER 4: 'Come on. Group hug. You too, Anger.' Joy, *Inside Out*. (Pixar 2015) https://www.youtube.com/watch?v=E41kD9lLtX4

CHAPTER 5: 'Nobody should be ashamed. Everyone's situations are different, upbringings are different, communities are different.' Marcus Rashford, footballer. https://www.gq-magazine.co.uk/lifestyle/article/marcus-rashford-interview-2020

CHAPTER 6: 'You never really understand a person until you consider things from his point of view.' *To Kill a Mocking Bird* by Harper Lee (J. B. Lippincott & Co.: 1960)

CHAPTER 7: 'There's no place like home. There's no place like home.' Dorothy, *The Wizard of Oz* (1939)
https://www.youtube.com/watch?v=LT12WuZb_DU

CHAPTER 8: 'There's not a word yet for old friends who've just met.' 'I'm Going to go Back There Someday.' *The Muppet Movie* (1979) https://www.youtube.com/watch?v=ryEjm3k6uY0

CHAPTER 9: 'We have an opportunity to create the future and decide what that's like.' Dr Mae C. Jemison, Astronaut & Scientist, speaking at The Makers' Conference 2014. https://thenextweb.com/insider/2014/02/13/astronaut-mae-jemison-interstellar-travel-cant-just-half-population/

CHAPTER 10: 'We do not need magic to transform our world. We carry all the power we need inside ourselves already.' J.K. Rowling (2008) Harvard Address. https://news.harvard.edu/gazette/story/2008/06/text-of-j-k-rowling-speech/

CONCLUSION: 'You're off to Great Places! Today is your day! Your mountain is waiting, So ... get on your way!' *Oh, The Places You'll Go!* by Dr Seuss (Random House: 1990)

Mind the Gap story – our version! (page 74)

Once upon a time there was <u>an astronaut</u> who loved to play chess. But the <u>astronaut</u> was sad because <u>she didn't have anyone to play with</u>. One day she met <u>an alien</u> who was sad because <u>he couldn't get back to his planet</u>.

'Don't worry!' said the <u>astronaut</u>. 'I can help you by <u>flying you home in my rocket</u>.'

The <u>alien</u> was so happy. 'And I can help you too!' he said. '<u>Because I am an alien chess champion!</u>'

And so they all lived <u>adventurously</u> ever after.

Thinking Differently (page 99)

1. It's illegal to chew gum in Singapore because when it was spat out on the ground (eugh!) it stuck to pavements and was costing hundreds of thousands of pounds a year to clear up.

2. The Dubai government thinks dirty cars spoil the look of their beautiful city.

3. Germany believes Sunday should be a peaceful, quiet day for everyone to relax, so no noisy DIY is allowed.

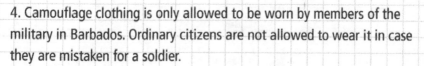

4. Camouflage clothing is only allowed to be worn by members of the military in Barbados. Ordinary citizens are not allowed to wear it in case they are mistaken for a soldier.

5. A whole salmon is a very expensive fish. This law is intended to stop people stealing them out of rivers!